*Paul writes that we are more than conquerors. Nice words. [?]
what does that look like as you crawl through one of life's inevita[?]
long, dark and cold valleys with only an infrequent flicker of lig[?]
at the end? What difference do faith and friendships make du[?]
ing trials for which no end is in sight? In* Letters for Lizzie, *Ji[?]
O'Donnell has given us a generous gift in showing us what it look[?]
like to meaningfully embrace the enormity of human suffering an[?]
at the same time experience the significance of God's sovereignt[?]
This book isn't just for those who are facing a serious challenge[?]
but for anyone who needs some real life encouragement and a renewal of perspective. If you are weary of pie-in-the-sky platitudes
or superficial solutions, this book will be a breath of fresh air.*

—Gary J. Oliver, Ph.D., is executive director of
The Center for Marriage & Family Studies and
professor of Psychology and Practical Theology
at John Brown University and the co-author of
Raising Sons and Loving It!

Generously funded by the

Canadian
Breast Cancer
Foundation
Ontario Chapter

in partnership with the Huron Cancer Prevention and Early
Detection Network

A STORY OF LOVE, FRIENDSHIP
AND A BATTLE FOR LIFE

LETTERS
for
LIZZIE

JAMES O'DONNELL

NORTHFIELD PUBLISHING
CHICAGO

All Scripture quotations, unless otherwise indicated, are taken from the
Holy Bible: New International Version®. NIV®. Copyright © 1973, 1978,
1984 by International Bible Society. Used by permission of Zondervan
Publishing House. All rights reserved.

Scripture quotations marked THE MESSAGE are from *The Message*, copyright © by Eugene H. Peterson 1993, 1994, 1995, 1996, 2000, 2001, 2002.
Used by permission of NavPress Publishing Group. All rights reserved.

Scripture quotations marked NASB are taken from the *New American Stan-
dard Bible*. copyright ©The Lockman Foundation, 1960, 1962, 1963, 1968,
1971, 1972, 1973, 1975, 1977, 1995. Used by Permission.

Library of Congress Cataloging-in-Publication Data

O'Donnell, James, 1948-
    Letters for Lizzie: a story of faith, friendship, and a battle for life /
by James O'Donnell.
        p. cm.
    ISBN 1-881273-01-6
    1. O'Donnell, James, 1948-——Correspondence. 2. O'Donnell,
Lizzie—Health. 3. Breast—Cancer—Religious aspects—Christianity.
4. Heart—Diseases—Religious Aspects—Christianity. I. Title.

BV4910.33.O45 2004
248.8'619699449—dc22

                                                          2003027354

1 3 5 7 9 10 8 6 4 2
Printed in the United States of America

For Lizzie,
whose love and courage have been never-
ending sources of strength and hope

"Our cause is never more in danger than when a human, no longer desiring, but still intending, to do our Enemy's will, looks round upon a universe from which every trace of Him seems to have vanished, and asks why he has been forsaken, and still obeys."

C. S. Lewis, *The Screwtape Letters*, Letter VIII

CONTENTS

INTRODUCTION

Life is dangerous.

Do what we may, live as well as we can. Wear your seat belt. Eat the right foods. Exercise regularly. Get enough sleep. Watch your weight. Stay away from bad stress.

Still, life can be dangerous. Unfair, too. True, the curse of rheumatic fever may break the hearts of fewer mothers in America than once it did. Sailors rarely die today of scurvy. Tuberculosis kills few in the West, and mosquito bites rarely cause death from yellow fever where I live.

But life is still dangerous for rich and poor alike, for the powerful and the unsung, even if its dangers are kept out of earshot of polite conversation. Illness still kills prematurely. Accidents snuff out the brightest of lives. Blisters from playing tennis killed a U.S. president's child as late as the 1920s. The Kennedys, for all their wealth and connections, could not stop a miscarriage in the '50s, spare the life of a son born prematurely in the '60s, nor save a president on a beautiful fall day in November of 1963. Nor, in 1999, could another Kennedy son see through the fog over Cape Cod well enough to steer his plane to safety. Life may seem safe, but it is not ours to control.

I know that now—but I hadn't always thought so.

I'd once thought that if I were careful, lived right, loved God, and showed kindness to my neighbor that an invisible hedge would grow up to protect me, and that the worst life could throw at someone would somehow be kept from my door.

But I learned that loving God, doing good, and loving others provides no guarantees that tragedy will not strike me. In fact, I learned that sometimes in seeking to be a blessing, one may become all the more attractive a target for evil.

In summer 1994, our family moved from Boston to Huntington, Indiana, 852 miles as the moving van clocked it, a move of immense social and cultural distances.

And change.

Nine years earlier, I had experienced a different change, not of mere address, but a "change of heart"—a euphemistic way of describing a profound spiritual and religious upheaval that turned me inside out and upside down. I had thought I was on my way to divorcing Lizzie, my wife of then fourteen years. But, as John Lennon once said, "Life is what happens when you have other plans." I'd planned on leaving Lizzie for no better reason than that I wasn't wildly fulfilled. Mine was, as I look back, a shameful and cowardly reason to leave anyone, let alone a wife of many years who had stood by me and with whom I had borne two boys.

But the divorce didn't happen. Instead, I met God.

For nine years after my somewhat-changed state had begun, I continued to work in New York and, later, Boston with some of the nation's top financial services firms, places like Fidelity and Scudder. I had even risen—in spite of "the change" —to become an executive vice president with Fidelity. But my heart was no longer fully engaged in the financial services business. No, I wasn't aching to work for Mother Teresa, but I wanted to do something more than just increase my own bottom line. More and more, I felt I was only making rich people richer. Good work, if you can find it. But I wanted more, crazy as that may seem.

I was in no hurry. I saw what I was doing as useful enough. Useful to clients; useful to fellow employees, especially my "underlings." I was a bit of a different boss. In my somewhat-changed state, we still had goals to meet, but I became a more caring person, rather than merely the clever person I had been. I continued to serve my employers, but profit maximization was no longer my highest ideal.

So I waited. And continued to try to give glory to God where I had been planted.

In that waiting, I wrote and spoke a little on college campuses and elsewhere about business and ethics and the spiritual changes that can come to a businessman, even in the twentieth century. And then along came an opportunity to teach at a small, one hundred-year-old Christian liberal arts college in Indiana.

By summer 1994, after more than a year of fussing over our pending move, our house in suburban Boston was sold, and we were packed and ready to go.

So we went—all five of us. Lizzie and I; Nick, our eighteen-year-old heading off to college in a month; Andrew, our fifteen-year-old, who hated us for moving him and, as he told us, "destroying his financial security with the dumbest move a father could ever make." And Jonny, age six, happy as long as Mommy was in sight.

I thought for sure the hardest issue we'd face would be getting used to living on a fifth of our former income. I also feared the cultural vacuum I suspected was ahead. The image I, like many who think bicoastally, had of Indiana was as a place to fly over or maybe to change planes on your way else-where. Hardly a place to live.

How wrong I was.

Within a few months of our arrival in Indiana, Lizzie was diagnosed with advanced breast cancer and given months to live.

What follows is a collection of letters written initially to friends back East in an attempt to build a prayer network to wage war for Lizzie's life in our new home. The letters were written to about two hundred friends and acquaintances, some of whom thought we were crazy, others of whom thought we were courageous. What they did have in common, for the most part, was that they did not share our faith. Most of them, in fact, expressed little religious belief.

When I wrote each of these letters, I didn't know if Lizzie

would be alive in a year. She was not supposed to be. Nor, I confess, did I know whether a prayer network would influence her outcome. As a still-young believer—after all, I was only 9, spiritually speaking—I had heard of such networks, and I was going to see if God might not help me create one.

Our friends back East responded, as did others who were forwarded our letters. Our mailing list grew to hundreds. Miraculously, and against doctors' expectations, Lizzie made it a year. But, along the way, she suffered end-stage heart failure that took us into another frightening world: that of organ transplantation.

The letters continued. The prayer network grew.

Lizzie has remained alive longer than many ever thought she would. But healing—that is, healing in the way I hoped God would answer our prayers—was not what happened.

These letters, and their retrospectives, which I call "looking backs," may trouble some. Religious people will differ on whether we can fight with God in our suffering. They may even more doubt the wisdom of fighting out loud. Many hold a notion of God that says He listens only to those who are just and good. Therefore, if your prayers go unanswered, your faith—or your prayers—must not be very good. Or, worse, maybe you're not very good. Illness can, to some, be the judgment of a just God.

And it may be in some cases.

But life-threatening illnesses and serious accidents will find us all in time, some sooner than others. Tragedy doesn't

discriminate between those with faith and those without, between "good people" and "bad people." Those who have suffered—and many have suffered worse than we have—as well
as those who have not yet suffered greatly, are linked. Some
of us may be assigned the suffering, while others, for now, are
assigned the caring. But all of us can reflect on the meaning
of that suffering.

We need to ponder such mystery. In our "feel-good" culture, where TV often covers the road between tragedy and
triumph in under an hour, even fitting in a laugh or two, the
irreplaceably central role of the Cross, of suffering itself, is
marginalized in our lives. In an age that also encourages us to
feel like victims if we suffer from receding hairlines or pre-
mature wrinkles, we want to keep life "light." Lots of us crave
to be entertained or have our emotions tickled. Maybe, if we're
lucky, we will keep suffering at bay, or at least in someone
else's yard. Yet, as surely as each of us will be older tomorrow,
every one of us will, one day, travel suffering's pathways.

These letters, written at some of the darkest moments in
our lives, offer a map of sorts, or maybe a beginner's vocabulary for those who have traveled through the Valley of the
Shadow of Death, as well as those who might be curious about
what it looks like. Those of us with faith don't like to linger
in those dark regions. We want to conquer the pain and move
along to the victory tales. But in so doing, we can trivialize
the enormity of the suffering that is, all the time, taking place
around us and in our midst.

Underneath a mature faith must be the certainty that God

loves us, cares about us, and is competent to help us in our hour of need. But those certainties are often shrouded in the midst of our suffering.

May these letters give you hope amidst your darkest fear. May you find strength in connecting with others who will love you at your worst hour; and may you, in the strange darkness that life can send, find the outstretched hand of the most powerful Unseen.

Letter One
Christmas 1994

LOOKING BACK
ON LETTER ONE

In fall 1994, we were a family that had just moved to Indiana. We didn't move because I got a big promotion and a larger job. We moved because for some years I had been struggling with what becoming a person of faith (which I became in 1985) might mean, over time, for me and for my family. I did not want to impose the effects of my inner struggles on my family, but for nine years after this change, I had continued working with rich people, trying to make them richer.

Before 1985, my profession had not been a problem. In fact, it was good work—high paying, filled with interesting people. But after 1985, I wondered if my work was the highest and best choice I could make for God in return for blessings He had been showering on me my entire life. God's claim on my life, and my response, were new realizations for me to ponder. I pondered them a lot.

Lizzie pondered along with me, but more as a loyal, loving wife than as someone drawn to reconsider her own career choices.

Out of this turmoil, lasting several years, came the decision to move to Indiana, with our three boys, a big pay cut, a house that needed renovation, and an occasional sense that we were making a big mistake.

In early December, Lizzie discovered a lump in her breast —perhaps every woman's worst nightmare—while showering. But there is no mention of that on the surface of this newsy letter describing our first fall in our new home. Frankly, Lizzie didn't mention the lump to me, either, at least not right away. She hoped it was just a temporary change in a healthy woman's ever-changing body.

Our house was in the most chaotic throes of renovation. One child, in particular, was struggling with the adjustment to Indiana. Still, for all the upset, life was still manageable. Life was still good.

Like a little family in Hiroshima just before the atom bomb was dropped, we were caught up in our daily joys and struggles, unsuspecting of what was just ahead.

Dear Friends,

Over the years, like you, we've gotten our share of "form letter" Christmas greetings. I never had a hankering to try one for our own family, but we've been asked a particular question so often this year that I feel the need to try to put some thoughts to paper for many back East. The question: "Why did you move to Indiana?"

As most of you know, we sold our home and I quit my real job in July to take a teaching position at Huntington College, in Huntington, Indiana. The college is a small coed Christian liberal arts school, almost one hundred years old. I'm a business professor in a department of five, teaching, among other things, marketing, global economics, advertising, human resource management, and ethics. The position I have taken actually arose some time earlier, but it took us lots of time to evaluate and pray through this opportunity.

To many it is hardly an opportunity at all. In truth, it represents an 80 percent pay cut and an uprooting of major proportions for the whole family. There is new scenery (with lots of flat land and cornfields); sunrises that now occur at about 8 A.M.; many people who find a really good time to be a meal at a fast-food restaurant; a house (a 110-year-old Victorian on "Main St.") that refuses having done with renovation and workmen; and many students who are the first members of their families ever to go to college. After college, a surprising number are thinking of "serving others" in various lofty and mundane careers. It is a privilege to be a part of this place and its work.

But this is a strange new opportunity to embark upon at age forty-six (forty-two for Lizzie). There's a bit of madness in it. Yet it had been coming for years. The truth is that I had run out of gas in corporate life. The tension between the values I want my life to stand for and what I increasingly found esteemed in corporate America just became too great. Besides, I know I was becoming less and less effective in getting my tasks done. I'm grateful for the time I spent in corporate life. It has provided much of the means for us to undertake this mad experiment. I met and came to know many wonderful people who remain in that world and whom I hope to see again, or at least stay in touch with.

But there is a new life for us here, filled with work and goals that are simpler, more direct and more closely tied to investing oneself in the lives of others. We didn't come here to make money. We came here to serve. We came as an outgrowth of some earlier decisions made in our spiritual lives, which later suggested—not demanded—that we take such a step of faith, not knowing for sure how it would all turn out.

So far, it's been wonderful. I'm blessed to be married to a woman who, seemingly, is ready to follow me to the ends of the earth and, maybe more blessedly, shares so much of my vision and values. I have not felt I'm "running ahead" of Lizzie, though I do confess to some guilt about asking her to come here in the first place.

Nick, who just finished his first trimester at Carleton, in Minnesota, is home with us for Christmas. He's had little time in Indiana so far. What time he has spent here proved to be helpful in our initial attempt to turn this house into a home, especially his first month here last August. (It has often felt as if we are actual pioneers wresting civilization in our house *from the wilderness.) He loves Carleton and is thriving with friends, schooling, and theater. Jonny, now six and in first grade, loves his school and has made friends well. His central concern still, though, is "Where's Mom?" As long as Mom is on his radar screen, he's content—in Indiana, New York, Boston, or wherever. Andrew attends a private coed day school in Ft. Wayne, twenty miles away. He loves it, but he has struggled more than any of us and continues to do so. He did the same when we went to Boston in 1989, so we're not entirely surprised, but we do wish so much he could "give it a chance." Just try. Be a more flexible individual. There's much to like about this place and its people.*

People have been easy to know and have embraced us all kindly. There's a lot of "dropping by" and other simple offerings of friendship. Restaurants, other than the fast-food types, are rare, but we've not been frequenters of fancy eating places, as some may be. Arts and entertainment have been abundant with the presence right here in Huntington of a first-class theater, arts, and exercise complex at the college that attracts a constant flow of "one-night stands" of marvelous talent.

Of course, only time will tell if this remains as good as it's been these first four months, but these first four months have also been hard to live through. Plaster, sawdust, messes—everywhere. We had no running water in our kitchen until October 1. Half of our stuff has yet to be unpacked because of the dust and clutter, and we still have a workman who lives (eats and sleeps) at our house five days a week. A nice man, but we're looking forward to having the house to ourselves for the first time since arriving on August 1. So as good as it's been, we hope it will get even better when this lovely old house is finally done. We're hoping this big old place will serve as a welcome "home away from home" for students and a more relaxed place to get to know them better. And we hope somebody from back East takes us up on visiting. (We've had one family so far.) We'd love to show you around Huntington—Dan Quayle's boyhood home. We could probably show you the whole place in about an hour, but we hope you'd stay the night, at least.

Well, that's probably enough from us. Life is good. There's a nice pace to college life. You can work like a crazy person for weeks, then comes one of the breaks, and suddenly, there's time to rest, reflect, read, think—things that grew increasingly hard to do at all in my old life.

God bless you all. Remember us from time to time. Call or write. We'd love to hear your news.

Merry Christmas.

Letter Two
January 28, 1995

Looking Back
on Letter Two

In early January, Lizzie went to Hawaii on the trip of a lifetime. She loves gardening and flowers, and I wanted her to go as a kind of "compensation" for having so cheerfully left all that was familiar to her back East. She went with some students and a faculty member from Huntington College on a ten-day, January-term course called "Visions of Paradise."

By January, Lizzie had, of course, long since found the lump in her breast, the lump that didn't go away and that she could not put out of her mind. By then, I knew about the lump too. She saw a doctor about it in late December. She was not overly concerned, not excited. She was her usual methodical self. A mammogram was done. Nothing showed up. But Lizzie and I both could feel the lump getting larger.

Then one day, from Hawaii, Lizzie called me. Amid

the small talk, I could tell my usually calm Lizzie was frightened. "Call my doctor," she told me. "Tell her to see me the minute I get home. This thing is growing fast." This was out of character for my sweet Lizzie who, over our years together, obsessed about others' well-being but seemed casual about her own health issues. ("Sweet Lizzie" is, by the way, a nickname I gave Lizzie after I came to faith in 1985. Like Muffy or Bubba, Sweet Lizzie is not meant to be cloying. It is simply what I often call Lizzie publicly and privately.)

I called Lizzie's doctor and set up an appointment for Martin Luther King Jr's birthday observance, Monday, January 16, 1995. We showed up early, and I hadn't finished parking when Lizzie came out and told me she was to go to the local hospital with orders for a compression mammogram and a biopsy.

Things moved quickly—faster than I could take in.

Tests and doctor visits became our life. A needle biopsy was performed. I tried not to surrender to its power over me. While in the surgeon's operating area, before he arrived, I made a list of house projects I needed to do. Lizzie graciously, or maybe bravely, cooperated in the list making.

Excruciatingly intimate physical exams performed before strangers followed. Then more tests and a surgical biopsy. My pastor came to spend some time with me while I waited through the procedure. I didn't know if I wanted him with me. His presence, comforting though it might be, gave weight to the reality that this was a serious moment in our lives. I did not want to grant the moment seriousness. I wanted it to pass away. I wanted to awaken and find it a bad dream.

I also remember the doctor who did the surgical biopsy on that gray January day speaking to me after the procedure. He came into the surgical waiting area where I was with others awaiting news of their loved ones' outcomes. He quickly eyed me and motioned me into an adjacent room that served as a small chapel. Later on, in many other waiting areas, I would judge the severity of many other families' loved ones' fates by whether their surgeon spoke to them in full view of everyone else in the waiting room or asked them to follow him to a conference room.

In our little chapel, we were alone. Colored light shone behind him. He was grave. He sat right next to me. He got right to the point: Cancer. A very bad, fast-growing cancer. He seemed nervous. He wondered what could be wrong with Lizzie's immune system to have allowed such a wild proliferation of cells so rapidly. I stammered, grabbing for control and hope.

"What about a second opinion?" I asked.

"By all means," he insisted, hoping, I'm sure, he could somehow be wrong. "You want all the help you can get."

Then he left. And I went to pieces. I sobbed like I never cried in my life. My body went limp. Great gasps of sorrow, so deep and genuine that I don't think I could have stood up. For the first time, the full impact of the danger of what Lizzie and I faced hit me. Making lists of house projects before upcoming doctors' visits would not bring the normalcy I craved. We were in deep, deep trouble.

In Indianapolis on January 26, we met another surgeon,

31

Dr. Robert Goulet, recommended by a good oncologist friend back in Boston. Lizzie and I thought it might be best to leave the Midwest and go back to New England where we felt the best doctors in the world practiced. Our friend didn't support the idea and told us that Indiana University Medical Center, about an hour and three quarters from our home, had one of the top breast cancer research facilities in the country. If we could get our files and films together, our friend would get us in to see the best.

Dr. Robert Goulet codirected the Advanced Breast Cancer Research Center at IU. With our introduction from Boston, I thought we'd get right in to see him. Instead, we waited two hours. I grew livid in the waiting room.

"I can't imagine we need this abuse, Lizzie," I remember saying.

Lizzie told me, "Let's see what they say."

Meeting Goulet, we brightened for a moment. We knew he had seen Lizzie's charts and tissue samples before entering the examining room where we waited like condemned convicts. When he entered with his entourage, including a medical student and a nurse, he smiled. I took that as a good sign. He made me less angry about the wait. His banter led me to think he was going to give us good news. We laughed together for a few minutes since we all happened to come from New York. And then, almost as if in midsentence, he stopped. His face grew serious. He leaned forward and said, "This is never easy."

I had to concentrate hard now to follow him. ". . . aggressive cancer . . . maybe a year ... I'm sorry."

I was glad, in retrospect, that I didn't collapse. I asked him, "What would you do, doctor, if this were your wife, and you loved her?"

"Try a clinical trial, I guess, if she were willing. But it's difficult with this type of cancer."

And then he left us to deal with the explosion, while a nurse came in and swept us up, like so many shards of broken glass.

Driving back home from Indy that night, we had a lot of time to think, to brood on what we'd heard during this life-changing day. We were told to take a few days—but not much longer—to think over whether Lizzie would enter the clinical trial. If Lizzie did undergo the treatment, there was no guarantee that she would get better or even enjoy an improved quality of life for whatever time we had left. In fact, right now, Lizzie seemed well. And if we had only a year left, with her odds for living so long, why do anything? Why not just take the time day by day, trying to enjoy each day as much and as long as we could? In any event, whatever Lizzie decided to do with the clinical trial, I told her I was thinking of writing our friends back East about this "adventure."

"What do you think? Could we let them know so they might pray for us?"

Letter Two was our great adventure's first letter from the battlefront.

Dear Friends,

*We're writing our friends back East and every-
where else to inform you of some momentous
news in our lives and to ask for your prayers.
Some of you may already have heard, but we
thought we would write to make sure the story, if
heard, is built on the same set of facts.*

*Our sad news is that Lizzie has breast can-
cer, and it is of a kind, we are told, that is dangerous, virulent and advanced. Clinically, the
monster is a 10–11 cm, Stage III, infiltrating
and focal lobular carcinoma. We hope that by
the time you read this letter, she will be taking
part in a "clinical trial" of new medicines and*

high doses of some older chemotherapy to try to get the cancer under control. If successful, in several months she will face surgery, more chemo, and possibly a bone marrow transplant. If blessed by God, this will be a long ordeal. Though detected as early as we knew how, the mass, in size and type, is very dangerous.

This news is so new to us that I think we are still suffering shock: how could something so serious strike so rapidly? And selfishly I ask, "Why sweet Lizzie?" Clearly, we don't know the answers, but we are doing everything within our power to get help. Our options are limited, given the nature and size of the malignancy. Indianapolis—two hours away— and the Indiana University (IU's) Medical Center, teaching hospital, and research center is a wonderful option we have open to us. Fortunately, too, IU's center is one of only fifteen in the country with an oncology specialty in advanced breast cancer.

We would ask you to pray for Lizzie's healing, even if you have not prayed in a long time. We believe strongly in the power of prayer, and we are trying to build the largest "prayer network" we can for Lizzie. We are not mad at God. (It is God who has given me Lizzie for the past twenty-eight years.) Our faith has not been shaken, though this is a time of severe testing. Having come here only six months ago, we had thought God's assignment for us was almost exclusively in the college teaching arena. Lizzie's cancer now presents us with a new, additional assignment that God has given us or allowed to be given us. We must learn how to be faithful people in this new assignment, one we never would have asked for but one that still can serve to bless us, our Creator, and others.

Yes, there is fear; there is sadness; there is a whole new vocabulary we are coming to know, one we never would have wanted to know anything about. There are lots of tears. But there have been extraordinary blessings amid the darkness. The greatest blessing of all right now is that, though we are told this type of cancer spreads rapidly, a bone scan, liver scan, and other tests done this week show no evidence of metastasis, other than possibly in Lizzie's left lymph nodes. Further, this community we live in—our neighbors, the college, and especially the church—have wrapped their loving arms around us in ways we never would have dreamed. We are, we feel, still so new here, relative strangers. Yet these people, by the dozens, have adopted us like storm-weary pilgrims caught is a tidal wave. What love we have experienced. It truly is the invisible love of God made visible in this world.

We are thankful, too, for a job here that permits me the precious gift of time, time that I can use to spend with Lizzie and be there for the kids—Jonny *and Andrew, especially. We're thankful for IU and our proximity to it and its particular medical expertise, and for medical insurance to help pay for the expenses ahead.*

We don't believe this is an accident. We are not living in the kind of world that God originally intended for us; and illness and crime and cruelty are just reminders of that fallenness. We trust in God's sovereignty over this world and for our lives amid this sickness. God can heal. But we also trust that even serious illness can serve God's good and holy purposes to arouse love and care in others, to turn our trust from ourselves to Him, and maybe spur some to reflect on what is important in life.

Letter Three
March 9, 1995

LOOKING BACK
ON LETTER THREE

On a cold, dark February 1, I saw my Lizzie off from the back porch of our home in Huntington as she embarked on the unknowns of her clinical trial at the IU Medical Center. It was 6 A.M. I felt like I was watching her launch into space in a fragile, unworthy space capsule, with little, if any, preparation for her hellacious journey ahead. A kind friend drove her to Indy that cold morning. I was going to go down the next day, after the in-patient chemo. Both of us had decided we would try to maintain as much normalcy and routine as we could. I would teach my classes that first day. Lizzie would start her chemo. It may have sounded cold, but we were learning how both to love one another and live under enormous strain.

The clinical trial Lizzie was enrolled in would expose her to, among other drugs, high levels of Adriamycin, a "chemo" drug that we were warned could, in high doses, have a lethal effect on her heart. Before entering the trial, Lizzie had to sign a multipage document that pointed out these risks. When a house is on fire, you can't worry about the car in the garage. Under Lizzie's circumstances, we saw no choice but to try the clinical trial. In any advanced illness, you face death if you do nothing, and you may face death if you do something. So knowing when and how to take risks—hopefully, intelligent risks—becomes a key to the fight. High-dose Adriamycin was, at the time, after all, in the view of Dr. Goulet, her "best shot." I remembered what he'd told me: If this had been his wife, and he loved her, he would have gone with this chemo.

But Lizzie's body couldn't tolerate the protocol, and with her white cell counts dropping to zero in both of her first two cycles, she was hospitalized twice in intensive care. Dr. Goulet and others at IU decided the trial intended to help Lizzie was killing her, so, regrettably, they eliminated her from further participation.

Letter Three was written just after her doctors removed Lizzie from the clinical trial. Leaving it was a blow—a major blow. Or so we thought. We both felt that, dangerous as it was, the clinical trial was Lizzie's best earthly hope. Now she had been cut. Did this mean she was only waiting to die? The question crept in, "Has God abandoned us?" Were her doctors only going to keep her "comfortable" from here on?

In retrospect, had Lizzie remained in the trial, I'm confident she would have died, since she later suffered "end-stage" heart failure just six months after Letter Three and after only two cycles of the high-dose protocol. Had she received the five or more high-dose cycles, as planned, she would not have lived long enough to find a heart transplant. But on March 9, we didn't know this. We only knew that what seemed our best hope had been moved beyond our reach.

Letter Three evidences well the faith both Lizzie and I were able to maintain early throughout the cancer treatments. We were under no illusions about Lizzie's chances, but we trusted that God was with us, that God had "not been taken by surprise" by the cancer, and that He would see us through Lizzie's healing or be glorified through her death.

She was brave, and I think I was, too, with an innocence that would not last through all the testings ahead. But in early March 1995, we didn't know what was to come. In fact, I was away from the battlefront, in Appalachia, on a week-long missions trip with college students. At home, Lizzie was in the loving care of her mother and trying, with a transfusion, to raise her blood counts to be able to take her next chemo treatment. Though apart for one of the few times during her long illnesses, our sights were still set on each other, on trying to be faithful, on enduring the ordeals.

Dear Friends,

Lizzie has now been in a clinical trial using megadoses of chemo for advanced cancer patients since February 1. Her particular response to the therapy, I am grateful to report, has been little short of miraculous. The tumor is shrinking substantially. The assessment of the severity of Lizzie's cancer is improving. Her survival probability has increased. Her likelihood of a mastectomy (single or double) has diminished now. This sounds and smells and feels like the stuff of miracles.

But Lizzie still has cancer. We know no more about how and why her own body's immune system was tricked into welcoming this enemy and allowing it to grow within her so large and so rapidly. (This was an 11-cm mass in late January.) At that time, Lizzie's surgeon, in charge of her treatment, told us Lizzie's cancer was "on a scale of 1–10, a 9.5 —a very bad cancer." On Monday night, he shared with her that in his career as a breast cancer surgeon, he has treated only one other woman who responded as positively as Lizzie has to treatment so far.

Still, Lizzie's body has, in effect, been hit by a truck. She is on a twenty-one-day cycle for her chemo treatments, and both times (she has had only two treatments) she has required hospitalization for five days, due to severe drops in her blood counts.

So while the chemo has been successful in working toward the eradication of the tumor, it has been hard on Lizzie's bone marrow. For that reason, the medical center will take Lizzie out of the clinical trial. She still needs the chemo and will get it. The tumor responds well to it. But outside of the clinical trial, she will get lower doses, and they will not be accompanied by the supplemental medications (in search of FDA approval), which work to stimulate blood-cell production in her marrow.

We still have a long way to go. While radical surgery is less likely, thank God, Lizzie is probably facing some form of surgery—and probably some radiation. Radium is no friend to bone marrow, but cancer is relentless, and you gotta do what you gotta do.

I hope in this update we all can look beyond the medical gymnastics and the rocket science of Lizzie's treatment to see the goodness, the kindness, the power, and the love of an almighty God, whose pleasure—this time so far—has been to show mercy, if not yet healing.

Don't miss this, please! Don't miss it, even if you give only mental assent that, yes, there is a God out there, somewhere. Make no mistake about it. We believe we are witnesses to a miracle, and though the doctors don't feel at home with such words, we hear them using words and comparisons that amount to about the same thing. Please don't chalk this up to thinking, "Well, they're just good people." Please understand: We're not! We are in as deep a need of grace and forgiveness as anyone who reads these words.

Please continue to pray for us. Pray for healing, and protection from infection, our own faith, energy to keep up with the never-ending family chores, time demands, emotional lows, fatigue, and consequences of treatment. May we remain cheerful, hopeful, loving, stable people. Some of you, I think, believe we're made differently from others. We're not. We hurt. We bleed. We get tired. But we get the grace for the day, just the day. And so far, that has always been just enough, just what we needed. So thank you. Keep praying and staying in touch. Be encouragers grounded in reality, if you can be. And, above all, thank God for the provisions so far. For without His pleasure shining on Lizzie's healing, we are, theologically, existentially, and figuratively: up a creek without a paddle.

Job, in the Bible, suffered much, but it wasn't until the end that he truly saw things rightly. "My ears had heard of you, but now my eyes have seen you" (Job 42:5). May we all learn to see God in our own lives.

Letter Four
May 1, 1995

LOOKING BACK
ON LETTER FOUR

As spring crept northward in 1995, people began sending all kinds of reading material to us. Favorite prayers. Poems. Stuff on vitamin therapy. Articles from *Reader's Digest*. Some helpful things; some not so helpful. All came as a result of love and concern. One enlightening piece that we would recall all through the ordeal ahead dealt with four qualities that seemed to separate cancer survivors from those who didn't survive: learning all one can about the illness, living as normally as possible while fighting the disease, having a loving network of people to support you, and maintaining hope. We seemed blessed to have all these, and things, so far, were going well.

Then Lizzie's sister Anne, meaning to be helpful, sent a technical piece on a long-term Italian study of women with Lizzie's type of cancer. I wondered if Anne had herself read the entire study and understood its disturbing conclusions buried in a lot of arcane medical data: that women with Lizzie's kind of cancer rarely survived long. Just what Dr. Goulet had tried to tell us at our first meeting.

With that article something broke within me. I feared it might be my hope. My successes in the business world had often been generated by bending events my way if I really put my mind and efforts to the task. The successes may have been illusions. But the odds of my doing anything helpful for my Lizzie seemed to be growing longer and longer—even with Christ in my life. Was there anything I could do that really mattered?

Were all the other women in the Italian study who had battled this kind of cancer pagans? Did God hate them all? Did none of them pray? Weren't any of them part of loving families that cared and prayed for their healing—and worked their tails off to try to get them the best treatment they could? Were all their doctors idiots?

Part of me clung to the childish notion that Lizzie and I were exempt. We were "good" people (as if other cancer victims were not). We could afford the best care. We would go anywhere, do whatever it took, to save Lizzie.

But part of me could not deny that this puzzle was out of my control, out of friends' control, money's control, out of Lizzie's doctors' control. There was no way on earth, hard as I might try, to have my way with Lizzie's cancer. True, she might be saved. But if so, it wouldn't be because of me.

I spent many a day busy with schoolwork and chores on our home renovation projects, trying to get lost enough in activity that I didn't think about the odds we were up against. Somehow, too, I had the notion that my work—especially on the house—would have a payoff in Lizzie's healing. How much, I didn't know. But I'd read that endorphins, those joy-producing chemicals in our brains that jack up our immune systems, flow best when we're happy. I wanted Lizzie's endorphins to flow like crazy, and if it took working like a madman at home to get rooms ready and pretty for Lizzie . . . well, hand me my hammer.

That early hint of discouragement does not overwhelm the hopefulness—or maybe bravery—of Letter Four but, looking back, a trace of hopelessness was peeking out underneath. The roller coaster we lived on every day was frightening. The ups and downs of daily life, waiting for news of blood counts, of Lizzie's weight loss, of my trouble sleeping and even just relaxing, all were beginning to take their toll.

Maybe because I came from a broken home, all my life I've been anxious to make things work out. Do my part. Act mature. I never wanted to screw things up, for fear I'd get abandoned for having done so. No, I was always the conscientious one, and always, since childhood, it seemed to pay off.

Up to now.

Now I was becoming an insomniac.

Dear Friends,

This is now our third letter to you on the course of Lizzie's breast cancer and treatment. We thank many of you for asking for an update. Until recently, there has been little to write you about since the last letter. We continue to desire your prayers. I think you will see why.

Today, things look hopeful again—at least more hopeful than on some recent days. I'm finding hope and faith are becoming the two most important weapons in this fight. All else, seemingly, is dwarfed in comparison. If we cannot maintain hope that the future holds promise for my sweet Lizzie, and if we cannot have faith that the agony of the treatments will benefit her, the best medical care in the world may be for naught. We are deep believers in God, but we are still human.

Since I last wrote, however, there have been days when faith and hope seemed in short supply. This path we are being taken down can get so long, and news along the way of any progress can be ephemeral or unknown. Conflicting reports and recommendations come along. We try to learn as much as we can so we can take an active part in evaluating treatment options. But some of what we come to learn frightens the daylights out of us. We're no experts, and some of the opposing recommendations even come from smart and well-meaning people, but we puzzle over what to do. Nevertheless, through it all, we've felt and frequently experienced the love of God and your love and thoughtfulness as visible expressions of that love. For that, we thank you so very much.

On Friday, April 28, Lizzie and I were in Indianapolis for the day for the first comprehensive review of Lizzie's progress and treatment since the cancer was diagnosed in late January. We greeted the day with trust and fear. I am pleased to say that the day went well, even better than we had imagined.

Lizzie's tumor is now approximately 5–7 cm, instead of the 11 cm it was upon diagnosis. Both the surgeon and oncologist are delighted with such a strong initial response to the chemo.

We have tried to learn as much as we can about cancer and Lizzie's kind of cancer in particular. There is evidence that survivors often share four factors: a network of loved ones who care and cheer the patient on, a developing knowledge of the disease that helps one take an active part in the treatment, the gift of not letting the cancer rule the family's entire life, and the presence of hope. We've been blessed on all four fronts, and I am so proud of Lizzie, especially in the second and third of those areas. But there are times, we must admit, when we learn things that are fearsome.

One fact we learned recently was that in Lizzie's case (of "local advanced breast cancer" or "LABC"— that's the 11-cm initial infiltrating lobular tumor), five-year survival was only 4 percent until a few years ago. A 1990 Italian research study of several hundred women pointed up that horrific fact. Cancer warfare has improved somewhat since 1990. Lizzie's five-year survival odds, by virtue of tumor shrinkage and current treatment, are now, we are told, up around 45–50 percent. Not great, perhaps, but much better than just five years ago, and certainly enough to fight this disease as aggressively as we know how. And we hope (and pray) in the immediate months and years ahead that progress against

LABC will accelerate.

No matter how much you begin to learn to prepare yourself for bad news or learn to ride the roller coaster of your emotions, news of a 4 percent survival rate just a few years ago rocks you. At least it rocked me, perhaps more than Lizzie. I lost sleep and found the tears coming back for the first time in many weeks. With the odds at about 50–50, Lizzie and I both feel newly invigorated for the fight. True, these are "only numbers"; they're averages of many different cases with many diverse backgrounds, care networks, treatment programs, and mental outlooks. You want to ignore them, but we've found it important, with all Lizzie is going through, to try to understand the best likely medical outcome for my sweet girl. We hope God will intervene to tip the balance in Lizzie's favor, but does that tip the balance against someone else?

It will be, we hope, a long fight—if God wills. Lizzie is now in her fifth chemo cycle of twenty-one days. This may be her last. The oncologist seemed to lean slightly toward stopping the chemo after four cycles, sensing the tumor's size may be plateauing, in which case further chemo is toxic without benefit. The surgeon, on the other hand, felt one more treatment may shrink the tumor one more centimeter, offering better odds that the surgery to follow could better target "breast conservation," rather than a mastectomy. Following surgery, which now seems one

or, at most, two twenty-one-day cycles away, Lizzie
will be exposed to more treatment—probably radiation, more chemo, and maybe a bone marrow transplant. We don't know yet. Cancer teaches you harshly
to think short-term, holding everything loosely.
Lizzie's hospitalization over Easter weekend was a reminder of how quickly circumstances can change.
But it does seem unlikely right now that we will be
able to get back East for a visit this summer.

But enough already. We continue to be blessed by
this local community. Did we mention that one dear
woman here took it upon herself to organize fifty
women to make a friendship quilt for Lizzie? Can you
imagine the time and love that went into such a beautiful work? Lizzie's mom—a dear, sweet mother, if ever
there was one—came in February for a week and has
been here two and a half months so far. What a blessing her presence and her ministrations have been for
our family, which itself has held up pretty well.

Flowers come from all over regularly. Elves bring
meals—now scheduled through May—and clean
this enormous house without my ever seeing them.
Honestly, I don't know half the people who do these
acts of love. And it goes on and on. Our medical
coverage, unlike the HMO we belonged to back
East, lets us go anywhere and to anyone Lizzie wishes. I have a wonderful job at a wonderful school
that gives me time to be with Lizzie, and as of May

12, summer vacation begins! Oh, how precious is the gift of time.

Letter Five
May 29, 1995

LOOKING BACK
ON LETTER FIVE

The spring term at college ended in mid-May, and then came my first summer vacation in a long time. In coming to teach, summer freedom was an unmistakable part of the job's overall attraction. Many of us lead such busy lives; free time is so absent. I know the rest of the world may not have free such a delicious slice of summertime, but at least I would; and I had come to look forward to it, planning to use it to read, travel, speak, and maybe even write a bit. But whatever I might have planned for this first summer vacation, it was unlike anything I had hoped. Like Pip in *Great Expectations,* who had thought life with Miss Haversham would be heaven, the reality was something far different.

Right after graduation and just before her first surgery, I took Lizzie to Holland, Michigan, to a famous tulip festival that's held there each year. We had a great time, with the newness of a long summer vacation upon us. But weighing on our hearts—at least mine—was the unmentionable reality that we were facing a disfiguring surgery that would change our lives forever. I felt like a man condemned to die at dawn. My sweet Lizzie probably felt the poignancy of a kind of final date as well, but she verbalizes much less than I. In a nondescript motel in Wyoming, Michigan, next to a Dairy Queen, I spent that last date having ice cream for dinner and loving my Lizzie for dessert. Yes, I was ready to do whatever it might take to save Lizzie, but I dreaded her breast surgery with special horror.

The summers ahead I had fantasized about—the freedom Lizzie and I would have to be together, to help others, to serve God. But also just to enjoy each other alone. Now all that might change forever in just a few days.

The trip to Michigan was like a final weekend in an old and much-beloved house, in which children had been raised and life had been lived well, yet a house that you will be leaving on Monday morning when the moving van arrives. What's ahead may be wonderful, but grief and loss have their place tonight.

As I look back on Letter Five, I look into the eyes of a brave couple facing down a relentless enemy, saying good-bye to a good part of their lives together, knowing the odds of survival are long, but understanding more and more that the race ahead will be more like a marathon than a sprint.

Dear Friends,

Much has happened in the four weeks since our last letter. Much is happening right now. I wanted to write to keep you up-to-date (so many of you thoughtfully call and write, and I don't always get back so well) and to sharpen the focus of your prayers on Lizzie's behalf. The prayers have meant much.

On Monday, May 22, Lizzie underwent surgery to remove the tumor in her left breast as well as the axial lymph nodes, situated under and parallel with her collarbone. There was good news (maybe even great news) and some bad news; but overall, God has granted us a miracle.

The good news is that of the twenty-five axial nodes sampled, ALL were either "negative" (meaning, they are now free of cancer) or "necrotic" (not as good, but meaning there is no living tissue in the nodes). This is wonderful news (I hope)! Its significance is in the fact that cancer spreads ("metastasizes") through the lymph nodes and the bloodstream. To use military imagery, cancer—the enemy—attacks us and uses the roads and bridges of the lymphatic system to access the river of one's circulatory system. There, it sends its hostile troops to far distant shores to wage war on other, even harder-to-fight fronts in the future. With Lizzie's nodes now all negative, it becomes unlikely that the tumor is actively sending any troops successfully out of its base camp any longer. Though we do not know how many may have been sent out before, nor where this (these?) cancer(s) may be now, nor if every last cell sent out may now be dormant or dead from five cycles of chemo, we have reason to be hopeful because of the negative nodes.

The bad news is that the cancer was larger than had been thought. During one of Lizzie's oncology exams during treatment, her doctor had thought the mass was shrinking from what, at first, he estimated to be an 11-cm tumor down to a more manageable monster of 5 cm or less. But the excised tumor was about 8 cm, and it did not have clean margins. A tumor's margins are "clean" when the excised mass does not have any cancer at any edge. The presumption is that if there is cancer at any edge, cancer is still in the body.

So Lizzie will undergo a completion mastectomy this week.

This good news/bad news scenario changes the likely outcome of Lizzie's disease considerably. For one, this monster cancer that grew so quickly and so large has now, seemingly, been brought under local control. We don't use words like "cured." We're not even up to "remission" yet, but it's looking more like that every day. To continue the military metaphor, it's about May 29, 1942, at Pearl Harbor. We're months past the devastating attack that took place while we were in our beds fast asleep. But we're in the middle of a war now, and it's far from over. We're up against a powerful enemy whose patience, wit, and viciousness have commanded our respect. With every headache Lizzie gets, I wonder if it's a brain tumor. With low blood counts, could it be leukemia? There's constant watchfulness and guardedness that no one who hasn't had a brush with death could—or should—understand.

That's something else cancer takes from you forever: a sense of innocence. A sense of safety that serious, life-threatening, mind-battering, heart-wrenching illness will not come to you, nor will head-on collisions, train wrecks, or plane crashes. Yet they happen to some. Integrating such long-term devastation into one's own life, while maintaining the essential goodness of life, is one of the great tests almost all of us will face at some point in our lives. We've just had to do it a little earlier than we might have thought. We are grateful to have the gift of faith, to believe amid the trials, the emotional roller coaster, and the setbacks, that we are in the hands of the God of the Universe, a God of love and mercy and infinite power.

What a perspective. We so often live our lives unknowing of how little we actually control, of how limited is our ability to protect that which we care most about—and those we love most. As strange as it may sound, cancer can become a perverse gift in helping draw two people—even as close as we already were—to focus on what is ultimately important in life and to see with new eyes the almost unbearable beauty and sweetness of so much in life that surrounds us yet fails to penetrate our awareness or to make us deeply grateful people.

So we are elated. We appear to have tied the score in the bottom of the first inning after the enemy scored twenty-seven runs in the top. Life will never be the same, but it is good. I may worry each time Lizzie has a headache or a stomachache, but we will learn to live through those times, trusting God to give *us courage and grace. And we will live as grateful, appreciative people of God, grateful for friends such as you and for each day God gives us, while we remain at His disposal.*

Through it all, too, we seem to be doing remarkably well as a family. Nick is in weekly contact and is appropriately, and helpfully, interested in his mom's health while his own studies at Carleton go well. Jonny tries to understand cancer from a seven-year-old's perspective. His most priceless remark so far: "Mommy, you're turning into a lazy girl. When is this cancer going to be over and you stay out of bed in the daytime?" And Andrew struggles the most silently of us all, asking few questions, trying to carry on as if nothing had ever happened, impatient that so much of his own life is on hold. (But he passed his driver's test.) Perhaps when you're sixteen and male it's a lot easier to express anger than fear.

Permit me one final thought from St. Paul, a remark he made in his Second Letter to the church at Corinth.

Remember, our Message [the good news of God's working in this world] is not about ourselves; . . . We carry this precious Message around in the unadorned clay pots of our ordinary lives. That's to prevent anyone from confusing God's incomparable power with us. As it is, there's not much chance of that. You know for yourselves that we're not much to look at. We've been surrounded and battered by troubles, but we're not demoralized; we're not sure what to do, but we know God knows what to do; we've been spiritually terrorized, but God hasn't left our side; we've been thrown down, but we haven't broken . . . we're not giving up. How could we! Even though on the outside it often looks like things are falling apart on us, on the inside, where God is making new life, not a day goes by without His unfolding grace. These hard times are small potatoes compared to the coming good times, the lavish celebration prepared for us. There's far more here than meets the eye. The things we see now are here today, gone tomorrow. But the things we can't see now will last forever. (from 2 Cor. 4, Eugene Peterson's The Message*)*

Again, thank you for your prayers, especially those of you who have told us you're "rusty" at praying (yet still praying) or "not very skilled" (but practicing). Boy! The God I've come to know is just crazy about those kinds of prayers and those kinds of "pray-ers." Really! No kidding!

Letter Six
June 24, 1995

Looking Back
on Letter Six

My beautiful Lizzie had come through her "completion mastectomy." Along with that, she had chosen to have breast reconstruction on the mastectomy site and a breast reduction on the other breast to provide some sense of symmetry. I went along for discussions on these matters because I loved Lizzie. But I hated every alternative to what had been my Lizzie. We were being pulled through a knothole to a place neither of us wanted to—or had asked to—go. It was painful. It was ugly. But absolutely necessary, for death still had Lizzie within his sights.

On a sunny day in late May, I showed up in Lizzie's room, after the surgeries, unsure of my own emotions, but committed to Lizzie. A young nurse-in-training greeted me with a novice's sensitivity and knowledge of nuance and insisted that Lizzie remove her bandage and show me, on the spot, her new chest.

Once again, we found ourselves at one of those unpredictable moments in the frightening unfolding of events and images in the course of major illness. Here, the source was a smiling, competent, pretty twenty-year-old, doing just what her textbooks and her teachers had told her to do, technically correct, but with all the emotional finesse of telling a three-year-old to finish his vegetables. She hadn't a clue of the loss that had just taken place in our lives, nor of the grieving Lizzie and I were then just beginning. But Lizzie dutifully obeyed, and I winced, invisibly.

Many women are rightly outraged that so many men think of them as just so many body parts—as pretty faces, breasts, butts, and legs. But as loving as I was of my dear Lizzie at that moment in May 1995, and as even more loving as I wanted to be, the loss of her breasts, as I knew them, was, for me, a big deal. To Lizzie, they were only body parts that had betrayed her. Now, she wanted them gone. Yes, I understood—intellectually. But, to me, Lizzie was and always had been so much more than her breasts. But that "so much more" always had included her beautiful breasts.

On one level, we had reached a milestone. The once-deadly cancer had, seemingly, been eradicated. That was a miracle. That was a profound work of God's grace. But the costs and the aftermath of surviving had aspects of surviving Hiroshima. We were alive, yes, and grateful to be so. But there would be adjustments. And even with committed love, these adjustments would, for me at least, in all honesty prove challenging, as I knew they would be for Lizzie.

I hoped I would always make the needed adjustments for my sweet Lizzie with grace and love.

And though I expressed hope that Letter Six would be the last letter I would write about Lizzie's health, I knew by now that such guarantees are not given in this world. Good health is only provisional. Still, I hoped that with all we had been through thus far, God might still protect us from further falls.

Dear Friends,

*This is, we hope, the final update on sweet
Lizzie's battle with cancer. We fondly hope there
will be no further need for progress reports, as
Lizzie begins her return to a changed but hopefully long "normal life."*

*As you may have heard, based on Lizzie's six
hours of surgery on June 6, we have some amazingly good news. Now, following a "completion
mastectomy" and reconstruction, Lizzie's breast
cavity is also free of any detectable cancer. This is
marvelous news! If, to the skeptic, it does not
quite qualify as "miraculous," it is, in the words
of Lizzie's doctors, "a surprising outcome."*

Lizzie has touched so many lives, and as I stand around doing my reporting, I marvel at the way God has worked with this beat-up but beautiful jewel. Student nurses have sat at the foot of her bed asking how she smiles through everything. "You're always smiling," they say. I've heard them. Lizzie's nationally-renowned oncologist remarked that he had just been reading her chart with reports by doctors and nurses of her condition—blood pressure, pulse, tempera-ture—and so forth, and he was struck by a line that, he said, he never sees in these reports: "The patient is smiling." For us who know some Scripture, I can't help but think of dear Stephen, the first recorded martyr for our Lord who, just before being stoned to death, stood before his accusers and was described as having the "face of an angel" (Acts 6:15). I know I'm biased, but I think in Lizzie's smile these wonderful professionals, these big "left-brainers," these techni-cians who sometimes see only sad cases and keep their emotional distance, these people are looking into the face of an angel.

So what is ahead? As I write this letter, I feel I'm writing something like a commencement address, marking not just the end of something, but more im-portant, the beginning of the rest of life. I'm struck by many things.

In the midst of life, we have had a brush with death. A car going eighty miles an hour brushed our clothes as we crossed the street. We're still stunned. We had begun to think there may be no tomorrows, so now that there are some, we're both having to plan for things that we had begun to put away in boxes and albums to store in the attic for grandchildren to discover.

Summer's here. We had written off this summer for chemo, surgery, and radium—hoping some of this stuff might just make a difference, always knowing it might not. Now, we are told, "You're free! Come back and see us in three months." Oh yes, there's a lot of physical healing from two major surgeries for sweet Lizzie, and in July, she is scheduled for her sixth, and final, chemo treatment. But about two weeks after that, we will be as free of overwhelming involvement in the treatment of cancer as we have been since Christmas. It feels, sort of, I guess, like winning the lottery. We are just beginning to think about what we're going to do with all the "winnings" that a good and merciful God, and the prayers of His people, have showered on us.

Still, we remember Lizzie has fought serious cancer, and while there is no longer detectable cancer in Lizzie, it does not mean that cancer is positively not there, or that it will never come back. Certainly, we hope it never will. But as I said last time, we may be only through the first inning. I hope the enemy will forfeit the game, given the comeback that we made in

the bottom of the first. But we also know that this en-
emy writes no resignation letters, makes no concession
speeches, and leaves no telltale signs that "he's had it"
for sure. All we get—and all we want—is the gift of
life, the gift of time—and we're grateful for that.

We may yet see some of you this summer back
East. If Lizzie does get strong enough after the chemo
treatment in July, we plan to try to come, probably
getting no farther than upstate New York; but who
knows, we may get all the way over to Boston by La-
bor Day. There are so many people we'd love to see
and thank face-to-face for love and prayer support
through these long, dark months. Some prayed "rusty
prayers" and some little prayers, some bold prayers
and some halfhearted prayers. All were cherished.

I hope you know how much that support has
meant—how much we sensed we were never alone,
never forsaken, never forgotten. If any of you undergo
a severe trial such as we have, I hope you will pray
and get all your friends to pray. We do not know
HOW prayer works, only that it DOES work. I also
hope when (note: not if) life gets out of control for
you that you too challenge the normal human ten-
dency to hide, to believe "no one would want to
know about my problem; they have enough problems
of their own." This is a trick of the Devil to divide us
and deny us the gift and presence of community at a
time when we need others' love so much.

Lastly, I hope this searing experience has nurtured in each of us our individual gifts of faith, be they small or large. Please don't forget, this was a very bad case in January. Today, Lizzie is, apparently, cancer-free. I hope this set of facts is not overlooked, amid kindly comments of how "deserving" Lizzie is of healing, of how good things always happen to good people, of how things "always work out," of how our positive attitude made the difference.

Lizzie and I feel deserving of nothing. We did only what we had to do, Lizzie especially, and not one bit more. Often, we have been hanging on for dear life, as if aboard the back of an open truck accelerating down a road we couldn't recognize. God and His grace did everything else: to keep us loving each other amid all the changes, to keep us willing to take the next step, to keep us hopeful that the treatments and procedures just might matter, to give us loving friends, to keep our family going, to send Lizzie's mom to live with us for four months, to give us a faith that refused to believe that God could not (and cannot) work through this, come what may.

Now, we end these letters with the opening words of Psalm 78:

Listen, O my people, to my instruction; incline your ears to the words of my mouth. I will open my mouth in a parable; I will utter dark sayings of old, which we have heard and known, and our fathers have told us. We will not conceal them from their children, but tell to the generation to come the praises of the LORD, and His strength and His wondrous works that He has done. (NASB)

Letter Seven
October 7, 1995

LOOKING BACK
ON LETTER SEVEN

I have found myself at some discouraging moments in my life revisiting the sentimental story of *Tosca*, by Giacono Puccini. In it there is one particular moment of such exquisite sadness that I doubt the heart of even a sadist would not melt. An evil official wants his way with Tosca, a beautiful young opera singer who is the heroine of the story. The official has imprisoned Tosca's lover and tells her he'll kill him unless she agrees to make love to the official. That choice proves too much for her. She swoons and, from the floor, sings her heart out to God. In grievous pain before her torturer, and in profound confusion before God—a God she always tried to serve in her life and in her art as a singer—she sings a beautiful aria. My Italian translation may be a bit rough, but she cries out to God, "Never did I harm a living soul. Secretly did I relieve many miseries. Always with sincere faith, my prayers in church arose. Always with sincere faith. So why, in the hour of my sorrow? Why, why, Lord? Why do You reward me thus?"

Letter Seven was the hardest letter I wrote. Life, as I knew it, had fallen apart.

He who, over years, had become the center of my life—God Himself—had, it seemed, become my enemy.

Tosca's words were also my words to God. My faith, like Tosca's, had not, of course, been perfect. But it was my offering to God, sincerely made, even if only as big as a mustard seed. And now it appeared to be despised.

In retrospect, I wish I could have had, at the moment I wrote Letter Seven, the faith of saints whose conviction witnessed to their courage and tenacity in holding on to a faith that held them. But I confess I wavered at this point. I was Tosca, lost in confusion, pain, doubt, and self-pity, wondering, "Where are You, God? Did You have to be so cruel to one who tried to love You so much?"

This does not mean I came to hate God, nor to disbelieve in Him. But my belief system underwent a profound metamorphosis. Whether I would find a more mature faith ahead, or whether I would lose my faith altogether, at that moment I didn't know. I don't know that I cared. What I did know was that the innocence of my first ten years of faith was over. And that innocence, for both good and bad, would never return.

What of my Lizzie's faith? During her fierce battle with cancer, I saw her faith waver only a little. She tells me I'm wrong, but I know only what I saw. And I saw a lot. For instance, one night in bed soon after her terminal diagnosis, she panicked, cried, and squeezed my head so hard in a terrified embrace that she hurt me. I have to rely on her memory to tell me when her faith faltered at other times. Such as the times she was hospitalized and put in isolation over Valentine's Day, Jonny's seventh birthday, Easter, and Mother's Day 1995. On Easter eve, she cried out to God to show Himself to her, in any way at all, to be present with her in her sickness, weakness, and seeming defeat, fearing she might die without seeing her family again. But nothing was shown to her that night, other than that she survived and lived to come home again. (On Easter morning a nurse brought her a paper medicine cup filled with three jellybeans.)

She also felt awful whenever she was hospitalized after sending Jonny off to school in the morning, feeling like a terrible mother who had abandoned her little boy, leaving him unprepared for what he would find when he got home from school.

But my faith never wavered. Not during the cancer, at least. It was as if some "holy bubble" had enveloped me. Outside, horrible things were happening to my sweet Lizzie and, therefore, me. But within my bubble, all was serene, secure, at peace. The Lord was on His throne.

My faith would return months later. But for now, I was in a wilderness—lost beyond any imagining.

No moment in that wilderness is so evident as one day early in October 1995, right before writing Letter Seven.

In late September, Lizzie suffered end-stage congestive heart failure, a direct result of the chemotherapy she had taken for the past nine months to fight the cancer. But we didn't know about the heart failure immediately. As September 1995 went on, Lizzie seemed to be getting a bad cold or flu. Knowing as little as we did, but being terrified only with thoughts of recurrent cancer, we thought she needed an antibiotic for her flu. So we called her doctors in Indy for a prescription. Hearing her symptoms over the phone, her doctors told her to get a chest X-ray and have the results faxed to them. Pronto.

Lizzie's X-ray showed an enlarged heart. We were told to get to a hospital and see a cardiologist as soon as possible. Lizzie was weak but relieved that whatever might be wrong was not cancer. We'd go to the hospital, if that's what it took to get her a prescription for her congestion. Hours later, during what we took to be a routine—and unnecessary—emergency room examination, a cardiologist told us Lizzie had cardiomyopathy, which means, literally, "death of the heart muscle."

Fed up with delays and medical personnel, and in a state of disbelief, I told the cardiologist I'd take Lizzie to Indy because all her care had been handled there. Dr. Rich, the caring cardiologist we would come to know so well, told me he wasn't sure Lizzie would survive the trip. He told me she "needed advanced cardiac intervention right now."

Horrified, I consented, along with Lizzie, to more procedures.

That afternoon, Lizzie became a patient in Cardiac Intensive Care at Lutheran Hospital in Fort Wayne. A week later, with the shock still setting in, I came home at lunch, made a couple of sandwiches, and headed up to Lutheran, twenty miles away, to see if I couldn't convince some nurse to let Lizzie be wheeled outside to enjoy a beautiful fall day.

When I first met Lizzie in the '60s, I asked her, like anyone in love, what were her favorite things. She said, among other things, "A sky seen through trees in October." This was one of those heavenly "sky seen through trees in October" days —cerulean blue sky, warm, bright, cloudless, trees ablaze in fall colors.

I did get an intensive care nurse to come with us. She wheeled the pole containing Lizzie's IV medicines outdoors, and I wheeled Lizzie—my lovely Lizzie, in a dreaded wheelchair, now unable to walk outside on her own. Once outdoors, I had barely opened the sandwiches and the two cans of soda when we were besieged by bees.

For a moment, I sat there on the bench, transfixed by thoughts of God's contempt, His utter, undeniable abandonment of us, feeling His scorn, His mocking hatred for us, malevolently conspiring at every turn to make life more and more unbearable. Now we didn't have just the likelihood of cancer's return to deal with, nor even end-stage heart disease. Now, with Lizzie's death imminent, God couldn't—or wouldn't— even protect us for a few minutes from bees so that we could eat a sandwich together.

But there was more.

Aroused in anger from my stupor on the bench, I, along with the nurse, wheeled the pole with the hanging medicines and Lizzie along with them back indoors, into the hospital's sunny atrium. No sooner were we there than a peace-shattering alarm went off that the hospital could neither locate, stop, nor understand. A voice came over the hospital's speaker system, competing with the alarm for our attention, telling us the staff was looking for the cause of the alarm, but they hadn't found it.

The world that God had made had gone mad, and I was lurching toward madness along with it. "God, where are You?" I wondered. Like Job, who never knew, had God made a bet with Satan to test how much I could take before cursing the God who had saved me and whom I loved?

A few days later, up at Lutheran, Dr. Rich gave me a prescription order for Lizzie, not for medicine, but for a handicap placard. "She'll need this, if she gets home."

I took the order down to the motor vehicle office and again made the acquaintance of a novice, someone who may have been expert in knowing the rules but was clueless in understanding the pain and loss that may be contained in a doctor's order for such a placard. The clerk typed away, telling me at the same time that the placard could be issued for only four years. After that, the patient would have to come in herself to renew it.

As I listened to her, I thought I had landed on Mars. I wanted to lean over, take her by the throat, and scream at her, "You don't understand. My darling may not even get out of the hospital, and you're talking some nonsense about four years from now? Are you crazy? Or, can you get the state to promise to make Lizzie come back here personally in four years to renew this thing?" I never said that, of course, but I thought it. I cynically wondered how Lizzie would make it to Christmas, let alone show up for the renewal of her handicap placard in four years.

I recalled what Elie Wiesel remembered of his first night in a Nazi concentration camp. Throughout his childhood, he wanted only to serve God for the whole of his life. But, on that first night in the camp, not knowing that he had already kissed his mother good-bye for the last time, as he saw flames and smokestacks he knew human flesh had been incinerated. He wrote in his book *Night*, "Never shall I forget those moments which murdered my God and my soul and turned my dreams to dust."

I, too, for just a moment, amid the bees and the alarm and the clerk at the motor vehicle office, understood all too well how and why Elie Wiesel had lost his faith.

I had started these letters ten months earlier to trace the yet-unknown course of Lizzie's unfolding illness, and, by so doing, I had hoped our letters might proclaim the goodness of God to dozens of people who did not yet know His goodness personally. When I began to write the letters both my heart and my will were fully engaged in a glorious, God-honoring work—come what might.

Now, my heart had disengaged. Only my will carried on the work.

LETTER
SEVEN

October 7, 1995

Dear Friends,

When last I wrote you in late June it was my hope that there would be no need for an update on Lizzie's health for a long, long time. Sadly, that is not the case.

Last Saturday, Lizzie was hospitalized in Ft. Wayne for what has now been diagnosed as cardiomyopathy—"disease of the heart muscle." She spent the first few days in cardiac intensive care. Now she is in cardiac telemetry, a heart monitoring unit. She wears a monitor there, hooked up to transmit and record every beat of her weak heart to the nurses' station with alarms to sound in the hallway if her heart should stop. She is gravely ill. Once again, we find ourselves learning a vocabulary we never wished to learn.

When Lizzie embarked on her high-dose chemo program back on February 1, we knew that the advanced state of her cancer at discovery necessitated taking some calculated risks. One of the drugs she was given to fight the cancer, Adriamycin, comes with known, potential side effects of causing some degree of irreversible heart disease in about 10 percent of the patients who take it. The risk is so well-known by oncologists that those receiving the drug are given amounts only up to a "lifetime" limit (presumably safe), which Lizzie approached in her treatment. As a result of the strong, successful measures taken to fight Lizzie's cancer, she now has a severely damaged, failing heart. Were it not for the cancer, her cardiologist says he would be seeking a transplant.

Her routines, if she comes home, will be limited further than they already have been. We will both need to adjust further and do the best we can to fight on, now on both the heart-front and the cancer-recurrence-front from her weakened position on the battlefield. But we will—as best we can, with God's help and your prayers.

This is a great blow. I say that still fully loving God. But God and I have recently had our quarrels (at least I have them with God). Today, one in eight women will get breast cancer, and of those who get it, only about 10 percent will have it in the kind of advanced state that dear Lizzie presented. Of those treated for advanced cancer with "Adria," fewer than 10 percent will develop congestive heart disease. Here again, Lizzie won a perverse sort of lottery.

For the past three weeks, I have watched my best friend in the whole world and the woman I love more than any other grow sicker and weaker as her lungs slowly filled with fluid (I wondered if this might be a metastasis in her lungs), as her breathing got more and more labored, and her energy ebbed. Little by little she began to die before my eyes. I looked to my God, my Friend above all friends; and as C.S. Lewis said in his book A Grief Observed,

> *When you are happy, so happy that you have no sense of needing Him, so happy that you are tempted to feel His claims upon you as an interruption, if you remember yourself and turn to Him with gratitude and praise, you will be—or so it feels—welcomed with opened arms. But go to Him when your need is desperate, when all other help is vain, and what do you find? A door slammed in your face, and a sound of bolting and double bolting on the inside. After that, silence . . . Why is He so present a commander in our time of prosperity and so very absent a help in time of trouble?*

Some of you may be shocked that I would cite such a reference to reflect upon my own feelings. But I love God, and I love Lizzie too. They're both equally real to me. And, like a brokenhearted beggar, I have gone to a powerful and abundantly rich Lord, who has shown Himself to me many times before, in kindness, in mercy, in love; now in my hour of greatest need He doesn't seem to answer. He doesn't seem to care.

Yes, I have those moments. I have known them recently. They are part of being human and loving the real person of God, somebody so real that I can quarrel with Him—afraid as I sometimes am to do so. I feel something like a loving wife, so in love with her husband that when he does something inconsiderate she grieves and pleads with him to change his mind. He may. But like any real being, He may not. I will still love Him. I will still believe in Him. But, right now, I'm mad.

However, amid my pleadings with God, I am not left without His insight and wisdom. One of the many treasures sent to us by friends has been Amy Carmichael's Rose From Brier, *a book written to the sick by the sick. It's quite a work, and it has kept me company on a number of nights when sleep does not come. In one entry Amy writes,*

> *Although through these months* acceptance *[of illness, disappointment] has been a word of liberty*

and victory and peace to me, it has never meant acquiescence in illness, as though ill-health were from Him who delights to deck His priests with health. But it did mean contentment with the unexplained.

Humanly, I still seek to understand the why *of Lizzie's suffering. I ponder a future that may not see both of us together as long as I would have hoped. Yet, I still trust that my Lord and my God will use our little lives to speak to others of the love, faith, and hope that is possible in this fallen world, that we may—even at so great a price—give comfort and challenge to some who don't fully know that, in spite of life's setbacks, disappointments, and tragedies, it is "a wonderful life."*

This summer, Lizzie and I saw the movie Apollo 13 *twice. It moved us deeply. I kidded Lizzie that she was like the ship itself, beautiful, magnificent, but damaged by a freak internal explosion, now limping home on its aborted mission. Like the astronauts, we tried with all we had, and all God might give us, to keep going. Our trip, however, would not last but a few days until we might attempt landing in the warm Pacific. Our trip would be of unknown length, and subject, perhaps, to many more onboard "explosions," such as we have just had, on our journey home. I was moved by the astronauts huddled in the cold and dark of their spaceship, hoping they might have enough power to make it home, if only they could avoid wasting the little power they had left. We too now cling to the little power we have left. But our power is not confined to a spaceship's batteries. It flows from God. It is limitless and forever, though we will only get enough for the day—and sometimes, of late, just for the minute.*

Letter Eight
Christmas 1995

LOOKING BACK
ON LETTER EIGHT

We were told when Lizzie entered Lutheran for half of October 1995 that she might not ever go home. She might die there.

Well, she did go home.

In fact, though our house was still undergoing extensive repairs, we actually had a sweet autumn together. Serious illness does that: It makes you mindful of what you have, as well as what you may lose. Simple things—like being together on a gloomy day in November—become precious when death hangs over you.

Lizzie had about a dozen oral medicines to help keep her blood pressure up, help her heart beat more strongly, help her blood concentrate toward the center of her body. We visited her cardiologist at least weekly. He was surprised she was doing as well as she was and saw the possibility that she might live five years if he could keep her medications in balance and if the cancer didn't return. Maybe during that time, he thought, Lizzie might even become eligible for a heart transplant.

A heart transplant!

I never knew anyone who had a heart transplant. Weren't they for people who had done dumb things with their lives—drunk themselves silly, fooled around with drugs, lived on the streets? Certainly not for supposedly good people like us who had money to take care of our health, send kids to college, give up the good life of New York and Boston to serve God in the Midwest. We lived charmed lives—or so we had thought.

But as fall wore on, Lizzie weakened badly. By late December, in spite of her wanting to be abundantly cheerful in our Christmas letter, she was dying again.

Letter Eight is our 1995 Christmas letter. I encouraged Lizzie to write most of it, since I had written all the others. But when she was finished and I read her letter, I struggled with the cheery spin she put on news she shared. I began to call her "Svetlana," because her form of truth telling reminded me of the way a Russian correspondent for *Pravda* might report food shortages in Moscow.

In the days both before and after Christmas, we found ourselves making frantic runs to the emergency room at Lutheran Hospital. The news we were getting there was not good, either. Lizzie had been hooked up to IV medications that helped "dry up" the effects of congestive heart failure, but I was beginning to see that she might not be able to live at home anymore. We couldn't keep her lungs from filling up with fluid.

Christmas was a dreary season for me. Nevertheless, Lizzie struggled nobly to fight any evidence others might see that her lungs were drowning in her own fluids. Unable to sleep myself, I might find her at 3 A.M. propped up in a chair at my desk with her head on several pillows, trying to find a position in which she could both breathe and sleep.

She couldn't find one.

Lizzie and I were beginning to grieve our situation in different ways, ways so different that we were not always helpful to each other. I wanted to talk head-on about what was happening. I thought Lizzie was denying what was going on. We coped so differently with our hurt and confusion. I needed to talk through the fears I was experiencing; she seemed to want only to continue life as normally as possible. I felt I would go insane if I could not process with her, out loud and often, the horrific changes that had occurred. There was simply no one else who could understand. But she said, "I think it could drive me out of my mind if I dwelt on what has happened to me." For all our love, it was a dangerous time in our marriage. Many couples disintegrate over the strain, because of the different ways in which we cope. Lizzie was forever trying to cast events in such a way as to minimize their hurt to me, or so she said.

"And to yourself, as well," I added.

Letter Eight, much of which is Lizzie's writing, shows that "positive attitude" (to use Lizzie's words) or the spin (in mine).

Dear Good Friends,

It is time I wrote you myself to thank you for your prayers and support during this past year of illness. But it is also the season of light in the midst of darkness, hope, and miracles. This fall I did suffer permanent heart damage as a result of aggressive chemotherapy, but I am doing amazingly well within my new limitations—my doctors are all surprised—and there is no evidence of recurring cancer.

I am a little slower than I was (yes, even slower), but I have been given the desires of my heart: to be at home with my family, to drive again, to develop new friendships, to garden a little, and to clutter up the house for Christmas. I am thrilled with this unexpected level of health and enjoying every minute. I know it has cost each of you dearly to ride this wild roller coaster with us, yet I am convinced that it is your prayers and God's mercy that have carried us through this ordeal so far, and I can't begin to thank you. The best way I know how is to share with you the wonderfully ordinary life we now live, which we no longer take for granted.

Nick, now twenty, loves his life at Carleton College. He's on a trimester system, so he is home, working at Wal-Mart, between Thanksgiving and New Year's. He does his beloved drama with great gusto and talent. We all went up to Minnesota in late October to see Nick in a run-through of his latest role, Richard III, *a big, gangly role for someone who is also a full-time student and doing his first Shakespearean play. But he was terrific! His spring trimester will be spent in London studying theater. He also plans to double major in theater and psychology, an interesting combination.*

Andrew is in eleventh grade at a private prep day school in Ft. Wayne. He plays varsity tennis and golf and has found a few extraordinary Hoosier friends. He continues to struggle with being in Indiana and probably being seventeen and the child of a chronically ill mom. He longs for the Big City (any city), preferably back East. The phone seems perma-

nently attached to his ear, and he is just starting to use e-mail (which explains our constant busy signal).

Jonathan, now seven, is . . . well, Jonny. What more can we say? He goes to the public school down the street. We love the school. Jonny has, at last count, 4,876 friends. Most of them seem to come over every day after school to eat and play. Jonny, being probably the only real Hoosier among us, loves all sports, but especially basketball. We have in our driveway a full-court basketball court—with lights! It came with the house. (This is Indiana, remember.) Jonny plays on a YMCA team here in town. It's something watching two teams of seven-year-olds on a basketball court. What a kick! What a joy!

For Jimmy, teaching college continues to be wonderful: important work, which he does very well, investing in the lives of others. If you hadn't heard, at the end of last school year, he, a rookie, was voted by the students "Professor of the Year." His large-scale carpentry projects on our rambling old Victorian house are finished, and we are on to endless painting and trim work. (This is Jimmy now: They even voted our house the winner of the 1995 Huntington County Beautification Contest—with an award of $400 in cash, a lovely plaque, and a dozen long-stemmed roses—a clear indication of their kindness and Lizzie's prolific design skill, since it was her color choices and period touches that impressed the judges.

I was just a worker, with help from Andrew, Nick, and more skilled craftsmen.) This "lull" is finally allowing us to have good nights' sleeps as well as to have students and church groups over. We continue to be overwhelmed by the lovely people here. Their goodness and their longing to carry some small part of the suffering still leaves us tearful at times. Why should they, or you, care for us so much?

That's life in Indiana! At least for us. It really is Jimmy Stewart and Donna Reed in It's a Wonderful Life *lived out on the big stage. And it still is, in spite of breast cancer and cardiomyopathy. God knew what He was doing in putting us down here. He has tested us to the core.*

A dear friend of ours back East, Elisabeth Elliot, has been another instrument of God in the "sustaining" department. For those of you who share our faith, you may know of Elisabeth and her life and her many books. For those of you who don't, let me briefly tell you why her life moves us so. In the 1950s, she went with her husband, Jim, to the mission fields of Ecuador to serve God. To serve God was their sole desire. Yet in January of 1956, Jim Elliot and his four American companions were speared to death. Elisabeth was left a widow with a little girl in the jungles of Ecuador. She, like her husband, had gone only to serve God.

In Elisabeth Elliot's A Path Through the Suffering, *she recalls her little daughter Valerie asking her mommy, in Ecuador, if God loved her daddy. Elisabeth said, of course, yes. Then why, Valerie wanted to know, did He let the Auca Indians kill him? Elisabeth could not then tell her little girl all the theology she knew. But she did want Valerie to know: We don't know all God's reasons. He does have His reasons, His reasons are loving; and not without purpose.*

We could not put it better this Christmas.

Letter Nine
January 26, 1996

Looking Back
on Letter Nine

Our oldest son, Nick, had created a calendar for my Christmas present from the time he was eight. Always, his theme arose from what Nick was most interested in at that moment in his life—baseball cards or candy or junk food, or houses we had lived in. Now, even at twenty-one, he didn't forget my calendar. But his 1996 edition was entirely on one single sheet, and in its center was a portrait of his mom, who, I felt certain, would not make it through the year.

As time went on, I knew less and less of the extent of what was really going on with Lizzie. She kept spinning what she knew from her own doctors. But as I stared at Nick's calendar, I knew—or felt I did—that on one of these days in 1996 that Nick had penned in with the precision of a draftsman, Lizzie would die. We were running out of time.

From our prior letter, written mostly by Lizzie just before Christmas, until this one, she had been in cardiac intensive care for almost the entire time. The congestive heart failure was advancing relentlessly. Lizzie could not sleep. She continued to lose weight.

She signed up for a January-term class at the college, just as she had the year before when she went to Hawaii before the cancer had been diagnosed. This time the class was on needlecraft. Lizzie went to one, maybe two, classes and then was back in the hospital. In the few days she was home, I remember going downstairs in the morning and finding her doing her needlework in the family room, near a window. She'd been up the whole night (night after night), unable to breathe if she lay down, she admitted, smiling. Cheerful as ever, she'd tell me she got so much done and she didn't feel so bad at all.

Throughout January 1996, our whole family and Lizzie's doctors worked on trying to get this young mother of a seven-year-old listed for a heart transplant. But no transplant hospital in the country would entertain the idea. It was too soon after her fight with a vicious cancer, and, ethically, there were too many others waiting for too few organs. And they were ill "only" from heart problems.

"I'm sorry" was what I heard, again and again, all across the country. "Check back in three to five years" was added by a few hospitals that meant to be more encouraging. But we didn't have three to five years.

In the latter half of January, another idea arose: the mechanical HeartMate—an experimental machine that could help the left side of the heart, the side that does most of the work, pump blood. The device might one day become "a bridge to transplantation." As yet, however, it was not FDA approved. So it might buy us some time, but only if we were lucky enough to become one of the few to get one.

We invested a lot of time—and hope—that January in getting Lizzie a HeartMate. Insurance wouldn't cover it, but we were ready to pay cash, if needed.

As yet, officially, Lizzie wasn't even awaiting a transplant. One day she might, I figured. So why give up trying and hoping, just because doctors and the makers of the HeartMate were being difficult?

We called the Thermo Cardiosystems' Woburn, Massachusetts, headquarters several times, had other friends call, and still others wrote them. The company wanted nothing to do with us. But our persistence paid off: We located one of their sacred devices in Salt Lake City, yet found we had no authority to buy the $45,000 HeartMate, even if we had the cash. Worse, word of my boldness was getting back to Lizzie's doctors at Lutheran. They thought I was reckless. One evening in late January one of the heart surgeons at Lutheran wanted to talk to me. Alone. He was upset. "You are endangering Lutheran's continuing participation in the HeartMate clinical trial," he told me. He said I might even be causing problems for Thermo Cardiosystems' application for final FDA approval. I admitted to all the surgeon accused me of. When Lutheran Hospital and Thermo Cardiosystems had said that no HeartMate device was available, even if Lizzie could be qualified to receive one, I called their bluff by telling the surgeon we'd located one. "It could be on the next plane to Fort Wayne," I said, "if you would sign for it and get Thermo Cardiosystems to agree."

The surgeon smiled. He admitted that if his wife were in Lizzie's place, he'd probably do just what I was doing. I wasn't the reckless nut he thought I might be. Before he left, he promised he'd try to get Thermo Cardiosystems to allow us to buy the Salt Lake device but made no promises as to what they would say.

"Even if they allow us to have it," he said, "first Lizzie will have to have a test to gauge the viability of her right ventricle."

The HeartMate could help Lizzie only if her right ventricle, which pumps blood from the heart to the lungs—a relatively easy chore compared to the body-wide pumping required of the left ventricle—was found to be undamaged and functioning well.

The heart surgeon thought out loud that the right ventricle was probably adequate for the implant. But still, first he'd have to do the test. If the right ventricle was too damaged, implanting the HeartMate would be deadly. It would kill her as soon as they turned it on. Lizzie would die on the operating table.

Letter Nine was written before the "big test" to assess Lizzie's right ventricle.

LETTER
NINE

January 26, 1996

Dear Friends,

*So much has happened since our last letter before
Christmas that we feel an update is needed.*

*Sweet Lizzie's condition has deteriorated
markedly, and time and options seem limited.
The problem is her heart. Throughout much of
December, despite her optimism in our Christmas
letter, Lizzie was suffering increasingly from
shortness of breath, chest pressure, and sleeplessness, all signs of advancing congestive heart failure. She was seeing her cardiologist frequently,
and she spent a couple of single days undergoing
tests in the hospital. Nothing was conclusive at
the time. But on January 2, Lizzie went back in*

the hospital, with clear signs her lungs were filling with fluid. With the exception of three days, she has been in the hospital since January 2. She is still there.

Her heart muscle has deteriorated to the point where it is hardly working. It is ejecting blood (a key measure of a heart's effectiveness—called the "ejection fraction" or "E.F.") at a rate of 15 percent. When Lizzie was discovered to have congestive heart failure in late September as a result of chemotherapy given her to stop the cancer, her unmedicated heart ejected at 20 percent. With two weeks of hospitalization and ongoing medication, her E.F. rose to 35 percent (normal is about 60 percent), but we were told the damage from the Adriamycin was irreversible and that Lizzie was then on a "plateau." It was not known whether the plateau would last days, weeks, months, or years. Now we know that the plateau began to crumble in December, and by January, even with hospitalization and constant IV medication, Lizzie's E.F. is down to 15 percent. There aren't plateaus under 15 percent.

The only long-term hope for Lizzie is a new heart. But because of her prior bout with advanced, aggressive breast cancer, there is no place in the country that will put her on a transplant list so soon after her presumed remission of cancer last June. Even if Lizzie were to get a new heart, the sweet girl has an enormous "immuno-suppression" problem to overcome.

When an organ—any organ—is transplanted, the patient's immune system has to be suppressed to get the organ to "take"—not be rejected. In Lizzie's case, because of the fury of her prior cancer, it is a presumption of all doctors we have consulted that Lizzie still has cancer in her body which now is being held in check—suppressed—by her immune system. If the immune system itself is suppressed, the thought is that the cancer will erupt wildly again, as it did in Mickey Mantle's case last summer when he received a new liver after battling cancer, only to die shortly after of a renewed and unstoppable onslaught from his cancer.

The best hope we seem to have now is to buy time, if possible, and to keep Lizzie alive and comfortable as long as possible. We may be able to buy some time through an experimental heart device called the Heart-Mate, now being tried in clinical trials with patients who do not qualify to receive a new heart. However, Lizzie has been refused entrance to all its clinical trials. So, we're trying to go directly to the manufacturer and see if they might give one to Lizzie for long-term use. By so doing, we would be pushing the device—meant only to temporarily assist the heart's pumping action —out into new medical ground. The manufacturer is hesitant for many reasons to agree, but as of right now, they have not definitely said no. So we fight on.

Obviously, we are not out of the woods, and I can see no time ahead when, medically speaking, we will be. We are both comforted by our conviction that God knows all about this. It has not happened "in a closet," nor outside His love and care. However, we do not mean to convey some Pollyanna-ish type of faith that Lizzie will be fine and we will one Thanksgiving Day look across our table at one another, look back and smile. We know we are probably facing devastation. We know the odds are long to get the HeartMate, that they are very long for Lizzie to survive long enough on it to qualify for a transplant list—let alone get a heart, which is another long shot; and in Lizzie's case, the immuno-suppression problem is enormous. Yet life goes on. Children are being raised. Love is being shared. Joy is daily experienced. There is grace. And we get it for the day.

Sweet Lizzie has begun the painful yet beautifully important work of saying good-bye to many who have come to see her or visit. There's nothing mawkish or maudlin about those visits. We both know beyond any shadow of a doubt where Lizzie is going, eternally speaking, if she loses this fight (sooner rather than later, or later rather than sooner). There is no fear; there is no dread. Yes, there is the immense sadness we both feel because of the joys we have shared together and the loss I feel in probably not sharing the future with her. As the illness deepens, Lizzie has shone only brighter. She inspires her doctors, her nurses, her family, her friends and acquain-

tances who come to visit. She inspires me daily. She is an absolute jewel. Nothing—certainly no "procedure," health issue, setback or outcome—seems to dull that conviction.

So we go forth together to face whatever is ahead, however long we have, thankful for what we have been given. Yes, we are, in a way, thankful even for this dreadful experience, because in it we have grown to know what is most important in life—not comfort, but stretching the soul; we have been tested; we have laughed and cried; and we've seen it through together.

When our third son was born, we were both believers in God by then and amazed by what God had done in our lives to draw us closer and set our hearts on fire for others, instead of only ourselves. With our first two boys (gifts though they were), we never stopped to thank God for them. But with Jonny, we wanted to thank God, and so we named him Jonathan as a commemoration and reminder to both of us, for his name means, in Hebrew, "gracious gift from God."

Well, the name "Lizzie" doesn't quite translate that way, but Lizzie is no less a gracious gift from God. I thank God for her, and I thank you for loving us, praying for us, and caring for us over the past year. Don't stop now, please.

Letter Ten

March 7, 1996

LOOKING BACK
ON LETTER TEN

If Letter Seven was the most painful spiritual moment I faced, Letter Ten contained the hardest human event to date.

Lizzie had her "big test" on January 31, 1996. The test was done early in the morning, at about 7 A.M. I thought the test results would be a foregone conclusion, a no-brainer. But as soon as I entered the room, I saw Lizzie crying— a rare event in itself. I knew the news was not good.

The doctor who had performed the test, as well as the one remaining attending nurse, vanished, leaving Lizzie and me alone with little more than her tears and her instincts to guess at what the doctor's and nurse's faces revealed. For they had told her nothing. Lizzie hugged me and said, several times, "I'm sorry. I'm so sorry," as if it were her carelessness that might have ruled out the HeartMate.

I was stunned but certainly not mad at Lizzie, as I

sensed she thought I might be. Did she really think I thought she hadn't tried hard enough? I didn't know.

Dr. Stanley Rich, Lizzie's beloved cardiologist, came by to review the films from the test. As I held Lizzie in my arms on the operating table and tried to comfort her through her oxygen clip, I could see Stan fumbling with the testing machine. After a few minutes, he muttered something about not being sure he knew how to read the films, and then he vanished too. Doctors, even good doctors, do not like being part of struggles once they appear hopeless. So Lizzie and I were once again left alone in a hospital room to look over the edge of mortality.

After Lizzie had been taken back to her room, Stan Rich came in for a few minutes. Like everyone else, I think, he too thought the test would be only a formality. Lizzie's right ventricle was surely strong enough to take on the HeartMate. It was hard for a right ventricle not to be able to pump blood from the heart to the lung, which is all it has to do. But by now, he had the official results, and, though they were not yet in Lizzie's chart, he came in only to give us the news. The official news, that is. He was tender, but, other than how long Lizzie might have to live, he knew he was delivering a death sentence.

Lizzie still considers that day her worst day. All hope was now gone. Her dreams of living longer to be a wife and mother —so important to Lizzie—were lost. There would be no Heart-Mate, no transplant, no time to see her Nick graduate from college or Andrew from high school; and Jonny would have to grow up without a mom. Lizzie was also struggling with not having time to prepare me to be a widower and a single parent. These realities grieved Lizzie far more than the fact of her imminent death.

With the failure of Lizzie's right ventricle now confirmed, she wanted to go home. After her test, Lizzie, who was so rarely unable, or unwilling, to comfort others who came to comfort her, disconnected her phone and requested "no visitors." As that awful morning unfolded, she remained quiet, even to me in her room, speaking to her doctors and nurses only if they came in, and only to ask one question: "When can I go home?" She didn't want to stay in the hospital another hour if there was nothing more anyone could do. She wanted to go home and be with her little Jonny, who found it hard visiting his mom in the hospital. She also wanted to get her house in order and her garden ready for spring. She wanted to spend what time she had left with her family, many of whom were now arriving to say a final good-bye. Still, Lizzie couldn't leave the hospital right away because she needed continuous IV medicines just to stay alive. It would take still another difficult week before a home-health-care firm could be located that was able to deliver the necessary medicines to us at home. Besides, even then we needed to learn how to use them.

In the meantime, Lizzie was given six weeks to live.

Again, heartbreak and a sense of abandonment by God overpowered me. We lived on a roller coaster we could not stop or get off—or control. And life on that roller coaster was becoming increasingly unbearable.

Doctors encouraged Lizzie to get her affairs in order. And

Lizzie, amazingly, encouraged her doctors. In one heart-breaking, yet funny, moment soon after the HeartMate fiasco, Lizzie saw sadness in the eyes of Stan Rich, so she and the nurses cooked up a little mischief to try to cheer him up. While in the hospital, Lizzie got many gifts. One peculiar little gift had been a sponge rock that looked just like a piece of granite—until you picked it up. Lizzie got a nurse to page Dr. Rich because, as she told him, "Lizzie had an almost unbearable heaviness on her chest." Stan came running. When the nurses gave her the word, Lizzie began moaning in her bed, "Help me. I can't breathe. There's something heavy on my chest." So Stan put on his stethoscope and slipped it under her gown only to find the sponge rock, at which point both of them burst out laughing.

"Oh, is that what it was?" Lizzie said. "Thanks so much, Dr. Rich."

While some surgeons thought she might have a few weeks, Stan Rich thought it might be up to a year if he got lucky balancing the right medicines. We trusted Stan because he was the doctor Lizzie first met in the ER at Lutheran Hospital the previous September when she thought she had a cold and actually had end-stage heart failure. Now he spoke to us in a more spiritual vein than he had before. Knowing my own difficulty in quitting, he told us, "Some things are just not meant to be. Fighting further would not be productive." I listened, and I finally agreed. We were done fighting. After a year of fighting, trying to outsmart a powerful enemy, we had to surrender to overwhelmingly superior forces. We had no more options, and we were out of time. All that was ahead now was a slow fade to black.

On February 5, we finally did get Lizzie out of the hospital and back home for the first time since early January. I came home from school that day knowing that the home-health-care people would be there to have us sign papers and sit through training on how to administer the IV medicines. The medicines arrived in small plastic bags, needing refrigeration and changing every twelve hours. Lizzie and I both knew that a slipup on one tiny detail could end her life sooner. During the same time that the home-health-care people were at our house, so too were people from the local hospice. The hospice people explained how they worked alongside the home-health-care people when patients were terminally ill. They told us about their own fees too, and wanted us, please, to sign here and there. They were all lovely, caring people, but I probably took in about a tenth of what they said. I had a hard time sitting through it all, taking in that my Lizzie and I were in our own home taking notes, or trying to take notes, on medicines and procedures that would help us make sure that Lizzie's life would end as gently as possible.

This can't be happening, I thought. Yet it most certainly was. And if the explanations and the demonstrations didn't get me, then the realities of our family's new life did.

One night as we ate our dinner, Jonny, still seven, started talking about summer plans. From the time Lizzie and I had been kids, we had each spent part or all of our summers in upstate New York. We had been fortunate to be able to have our own children know the beauty and rest that can come from a "summer place." But until that moment, I hadn't thought about summer and the changes that were likely in store for all of us. Lizzie was quicker than I, and she piped up, "Sure, Jonny, you will get to New York this summer." Jonny, knowing his mom was sick but not comprehending how much, wondered if she would come. Lizzie's eyes shot to mine, but I was tongue-tied and my eyes teared up. I knew if I spoke I'd lose it. Lizzie spoke right up and told Jonny that she might not be able to come, "But Daddy will go to give you a good time in New York this summer." I had to excuse myself, hoping I could hold back my emotions until I was out of sight.

How had this happened? I wondered. *What had we done?*

A week or so later, on the way home from a hospital visit to Stanley Rich, Lizzie ambushed me with a request to look at cemeteries and to make an appointment to meet with a funeral home. I wanted, now more than ever, to please Lizzie. But I told her I did not need to visit cemeteries or funeral homes. In time, if needed, I would take care of all that stuff.

But she insisted. She was firm that after all the trouble she had caused, it was the least she could do now to make her own final arrangements and spare me the pain. I felt torn, sick. Lizzie seemed to continue to look at her illness and its effects as something she had "caused" or something over which she could have taken better control.

I didn't want to argue with Lizzie about anything. I wanted to be a good sport, whatever she wanted. Though when she wanted her clothes out of our bedroom—along with her dresser—that was too much for me. When she wanted to look at cemetery plots and meet a funeral director, I went. I was there, too, when she picked out a casket. And when we bought a gravesite. But she had to make all the arrangements herself because my emotions kept me from speaking when she asked me my preferences.

No single event rivaled the pain of those cemetery and funeral-home visits. If I had to be face-to-face with Lizzie's death, I didn't want to do it more than once. Picking out a grave with her, and then picking out a casket, rubbed her impending death in my face like a puppy's nose might be rubbed in a mess he left behind. Yet I couldn't allow myself to deny Lizzie's wishes now.

Now, too, we were reduced to using a baby monitor, one of those things young mothers put in a sleeping infant's room to keep tabs on the child. We couldn't sleep together anymore —she couldn't climb the several stairs to our bedroom. Nor could I sleep in the same bed with Lizzie's IV pumps turning on and off every few seconds, sending their life-giving medicines into her heart night and day. So I borrowed the monitor from a friend at college. Lizzie would sleep downstairs, in "the room behind the refrigerator." If she needed me during the night, I could hear her on the monitor. I did not want her to die alone.

Again, we adjusted. We adjusted to whatever came at us. But oh! the pain I felt, as life slowly ebbed away in someone in whose eyes the sun had risen and set for me for so many years.

March 7, 1996, the date of Letter Ten, was also Jonny's eighth birthday party. Lizzie and I were sure it would be her last with him, so she worked to exhaustion to set up the games and food that his sleepover friends would share. Our family photographs of the day show her loving every minute.

LETTER
TEN

March 7, 1996

Dear Friends,

*Your cards and letters, calls, and flowers keep
coming. How grateful we are for the love and support we feel, even though we may not get back to
thank each of you for every gesture. You help so
much. You provide cushioning in what has, at
times, seemed to be a free fall into devastation.
We've had several inquiries lately that lead us to
write anew, to update you on what is going on.*

*In our last letter, dated January 25, we men-
tioned that Lizzie was trying to get a HeartMate
device to replace "half" of her deteriorating
heart. After considerable wrangling, we were fortunate to get a tentative okay to have the device*

implanted at the end of January if Lizzie's right ventricle were strong enough to carry its load. Unfortunately, the right ventricle proved to be too weak (a severe blow to us both), so the doctors and surgeons came to the regrettable conclusion that there was nothing more to do. On February 5, sweet Lizzie was released from the hospital, not because she was better, but so she might best enjoy her remaining time. Lizzie's desire was to come home to be with her family. She had seen Nick for a weekend in late January; Andrew is engaging his mom and her illness much more productively; and Jonny . . . well, delightful little Jonny lives as if nothing has really changed.

How much time is left is up to God, of course, as this whole ordeal has been under His providence all along. The heart-transplant surgeons who were going to perform the implant of the HeartMate felt, in late January, that Lizzie may have but weeks; her own main doctor, a cardiologist, hopes that if he could keep Lizzie's myriad medicines balanced she might have a year. Right now she looks and acts wonderfully. But we don't know what time there may be. As Psalm 31 reminds us, "[Our] times are in your hands."

Lizzie has come home with a disarming amount of medicine. She has two continuous IV medications that help her heart beat and constrict blood circulation to the outermost parts of her body. She has twelve oral medications to take as many as four times a day, some of which need rebalancing every few days. We have help from home-health-care nurses, not every day but several times a week. And through it all, Lizzie remains the picture of beauty and uncomplaining calm. (If you call her, she will tell you, after you ask how she is, "Oh, I'm fine!" It's not denial. It's part of her marvelous fighting mechanism. But it maddens me at times.) I can't say that either of us right now holds out great hope for a miracle in what seems the bottom of the ninth inning. We know God can and may do anything; lots and lots of prayers have gone up already in support of the outcome we'd like to see. So far, events have not gone the way we would have hoped, but we trust in a God who still knows best. We are also realists, in need of making plans.

Lizzie has had a wonderful and comfortable first four weeks home. She is on one of the "plateaus" we have spoken of before. It can last days, weeks, or months. On it, she is out of bed and with us for much of the day. Yes, she needs to rest, and no, she doesn't do stairs in a three-story Victorian anymore. But when we first planned this house, we put a guest bedroom off the kitchen, which we hoped would be an inducement to Lizzie's mother to come and visit once in a while. Of course, as events turned out, Lizzie's mom has become a virtual resident of Indiana, and Lizzie has become the guest who beautifies the room behind the refrigerator. Lizzie's days, while restricted because of medicinal routines and little energy, still permit her to be up and about as many as two or three hours at a time to be with Jonny and me, go out a little, and be about her projects.

During one foray out this past week, we bought a convertible! Quite an outing. I had planned to take Lizzie to Europe this summer for a twenty-fifth anniversary trip to visit some gardens. That trip seems out right now, whatever Lizzie's condition by summer. But last week we had a seventy-degree day. So I left school for a couple of hours to go for a ride with her, and it dawned on me that with what time we have, wouldn't spring be nice to share that time with Lizzie in a convertible? Now, of course, this is reckless extravagance, especially given that it is two degrees this morning as I write this. But for both of us, who have rarely lived with abandon, just this once it seemed appropriate.

Lest you feel now that all is sweetness and light for us in Indiana (in many ways, it is) and that you, too, should explore the life-transforming wonders of breast cancer and cardiomyopathy, let me share a word about Lizzie's "projects," mentioned earlier. For in them, we come to some things that have pushed me to, and sometimes through, my limits.

Sweet Lizzie feels that she is dumping a great load on me, so with what time she has left she wants to do what she can to make the uncertain future more bearable for me. One of the projects she hopes to finish is some decorating, getting a table for a certain spot (because she knows I might not). She also wants to finish planning out her garden, even if it doesn't get planted. Then at least I will have her plans in hand. These are, you can imagine, touching conversations to have with someone you love more than anybody in the world.

But when she asked to look at cemeteries, to pick out graves, to visit a funeral director, and (positively the worst moment so far) to pick out a casket—well! Words fail me. I begin to choke up. Lizzie begins to choke up. She wants to do this, she says, for me. I don't want any part of it, yet I want to be with her, to support her. I know she means to be loving, but I'm over my limit. So we go, and I cry, and she cries, and I get angry, and sad, and both at once. It's too much, way too much for us at such moments. While neither of us hides from reality, let me assure you, we try to go on with life, as normally as we can, treasuring every moment and every day we are given. But then we come to a moment such as Lizzie's trying to climb a flight of stairs and having to rest midway, and there, collapsing in a heap, she cries from discouragement.

I think back to all the events we, like many others, have had the privilege to share: picking out wedding rings, looking at apartments, houses, cribs, *furniture, kitchens, cars, garden plantings, and so much more. Now we are choosing caskets and graves. And suddenly, death, so intrusive, so belligerent, is in your face.*

Yes, sometimes we cherish the illusion that we will stay as we are now, on this plateau, for a long time—maybe forever. But then a moment comes, like on the stairs, that reminds us that death seems to be just circling the block. He has his orders. He's looking for an address. He's not going away. He's looking for a "pickup," and, in time, he will not be put off.

Speaking for myself, I function on two levels. On one, everything is going to be fine. Lizzie is set. She knows God. Her sins are forgiven, and she will awaken in heaven. But, on another level, the level of here and now, I'm brokenhearted. I can't help feeling at some moments as if I'm standing on a train platform about to send off my beloved for a long, long time.

I'm scared and lonely too. Yes, we will meet again, but the human side of me wars against the parting. It's too soon. It's not fair. We could do so much more together. Please, not yet. Please, oh please.

Letter Eleven
April 15, 1996

LOOKING BACK
ON LETTER ELEVEN

April came.

Lizzie was doing well—at least, for someone who had been given weeks to live back in early February. We regularly got calls now both from people who knew us and people who didn't know us but wanted to help. There were calls about religious healing services in this place or that. There were calls about herbal cures, trips to faraway places where we might, just might, find the answer.

Lizzie and I talked about these things as they came up. We were of one mind. We thanked the callers. We knew they meant well.

But our energies were much more limited now. We did not want to waste the last weeks of Lizzie's life on planes flying to see gurus or attending healing services or exploring herbal cures. Each, in its own way, was being offered to us out of love; we understood that. And each might have benefits that could help. But each demanded energy, energy that Lizzie and I no longer had. If God still had something up His sleeve in this, our ninth inning, then He was able, we trusted, to bring it to us without exhausting Lizzie by going too far.

As I tried to see our plight from God's standpoint, it seemed clear that we had done whatever we could. Sometimes, God says "yes," sometimes "wait," and sometimes "no." We seemed to have heard, in the events as they played out for Lizzie, a clear "no." And while Lizzie was not dead yet, we were no longer believing that there was a way out, at least in this world.

But something different from anything we had expected was ahead.

I cannot honestly say that at the beginning—even though this turning point occurred on Easter Day, the feast of the Resurrection—I sensed God at work. I did not want to get my, or Lizzie's, hopes up. By now, we both were resigned to Lizzie's death. Coming to that resignation had been painful, so I was slow to give up that hard-won acceptance, if later I'd have to relearn it all over again.

As events unfolded at great speed now, I worried: Was God at work in this? Was this a development that would lead us into new areas of hope for Lizzie's life? Or were Lizzie and I about to be lifted up, only to be crushed again? Or maybe, most fearfully, could this be something of both? What terrors might await us? How awful it is that such a thought found a home in my heart. But we had both learned to fear. As we saw the finish line of our second marathon, would we be told to keep running?

I wondered. And I hoped. But I feared too.

We were now so deep in the unhappy and seemingly endless progress of Lizzie's illnesses that I no longer prayed earnestly to God for healing—but simply for His protection from the terrors.

In the book of Job, sure that it was God who was behind his sufferings, Job pleaded in confusion, bitterness, and sorrow, "If only there were ... someone to remove God's rod from me, so that his terror would frighten me no more" (Job 9:33–34).

This labyrinth of sickness had now surrounded us for over a year. Its walls, too high to see over, led us to fantasize hope one moment and brood on loss the next. This labyrinth had become a wretched house of horrors in which, day by day, Lizzie and I were growing increasingly lost. On that floor of our labyrinth, exhausted from trying to find a way out, we awakened from fitful sleeps with no safe place to hide, imagining terrorists pointing guns at us in meaningless jest. These were the "terrors." This is what Job must have meant by the terrors. Strangely, early on, cancer had had its perverse logic. Now there was no longer logic. The bees of October, the alarm —these were symbolic of the stalkers who haunted us at every turn. Life kept unfolding in a series of losses, interspersed with crumbs of hope that, unlike Hansel and Gretel's path through the woods, led us only to lower highs and lower lows.

Now, as we faced the mere possibility of a transplant, we needed courage to believe this was not just another trick of "the terrors."

Dear Friends,

One of the hardest parts of living with long-term, life-threatening illness is the roller-coaster quality that life itself assumes. Something happens to lift our hopes; spirits rise expectantly. Then we hit another wall or wind up on a dead end, and our hopes crash down. Again. Preparations are made for "the end." But the end doesn't come, so hopes begin to rise once more. And so the cycle goes, on and on, again and again. The fact that we are people of significant faith does not exempt our humanness from being swept up into this twisting and turning human drama.

Therefore, it is with great excitement, and yet a large measure of caution, that I share recent news on the course of sweet Lizzie's battle for life.

When last I wrote, in early March, Lizzie had been home from the hospital for a month. Medically, there was nothing more to do, so Lizzie was sent home to spend her remaining time with her family and friends. Now, more than two months later, she is still alive and going strong. There has been no deterioration in her condition. She looks good, is up a fair amount of each day, and continues her many "projects," things like getting missing items of furniture for a room that I will not know how to complete or making waterproof nametags for her plants and shrubs outside that I will not be able to identify. She is still taking a veritable pharmacy of medications, as well as her round-the-clock IVs. But we have no complaints; in spite of it all, she appears to be thriving.

So it may come as no particular shock that in late March, we were apprised of a daring, still-experimental, but promising surgery called cardiomyoplasty that might be of help to Lizzie. Cardiomyoplasty involves taking a muscle from the back and wrapping it around a weakened heart. Then, over time, with a pacemaker, muscle is retrained to act as cardiac tissue. In the two hundred or so cardiomyoplasties that have been performed since 1985 (when first it was done in France), success has been dramat-

ic. However, the operation is not viewed as a permanent solution. As with the HeartMate we hoped for in January, a cardiomyoplasty is only a bridge to transplantation. It buys some time.

For a week or so, we went in search of a cardiomyoplasty and found that its U.S. surgical center is Pittsburgh. Over Easter weekend, we prepared to make a trip there the following week to have Lizzie assessed, but hopes were dashed when the premier cardiomyoplasty surgeon told us that sweet Lizzie's heart was too weak to undergo the operation. "She is not a good candidate," we were told, which sounded like the old saw about trying to get a loan at a bank: You can get one only if you can prove you don't need one. Sadly, it wouldn't be worthwhile even traveling to Pittsburgh to have her seen by the surgeon.

One door closed. But on Easter morning, through the kindness of good friends back East, I was put in touch with a prominent heart surgeon in Miami, Florida. Something came up in our conversation that I can ascribe only to the grace of God, which led me to believe there may be something new and significant about to happen. The surgeon praised the medical people in Pittsburgh (whose answer on the cardiomyoplasty we would not know for another twenty-four hours). But the Miami surgeon, too, pointed out that Lizzie needed a heart, not a cardiomyoplasty. "I know," I said, "but immuno-suppres-

sion is the problem." (For those who may not remember, immuno-suppression, or suppression of the body's immune system, is a necessary part of organ transplantation. But with cancer patients it can trigger a deadly reactivation of cancer cells' growth when the immune system is "turned off.")

The Florida heart surgeon challenged that, which surprised me.

"Who says so? Are you sure? Make sure!" He wouldn't give up. He was not an oncologist, he admitted. But if the immuno-suppression issue turned out not *to be the issue I claimed it was (because I had been told as much—often), then he, a virtual stranger to us, said he would personally work to get Lizzie a heart somewhere.*

Imagine!

The next day, sweet Lizzie was crushed by her failure to qualify for the cardiomyoplasty. Yet, that same day, we contacted Lizzie's nationally renowned oncologist in Indianapolis, wondering, yet again, in his educated view, how good a candidate was Lizzie for a heart transplant?

As was the case the night before, so too on Monday, April 8, we had a most unexpected medical conversation. The oncologist said he was just now getting results from new research that showed that Lizzie's particular variety of breast cancer posed no particular immuno-suppression risk. This was news to us, and it would be news to the transplant and oncological communities. Yes, dear Lizzie still has about a 40 percent risk over the next two to three years of her cancer's return, but the previous supposition that transplantation would heighten the risk of the cancer's return simply no longer was an issue in her oncologist's mind.

Wow! What stunning news! Life stopped for a moment when we put the phone down. A way through the wilderness may have been found. And would we have ever learned this had I not been challenged so pointedly the night before?

Needless to say, we are thrilled, and humbled, by this news. But let us also share both our thankfulness that we live in such a time when this type of surgery is even possible. And let us, too, share our realistic thoughts about what this means. If actually accepted as a heart transplant patient, Lizzie will enter Lutheran Hospital in Fort Wayne and stay there anywhere from two weeks to perhaps two months or more, awaiting a heart. She cannot be considered "extremely likely" to get a heart unless she is in the hospital, though we are but twenty-five minutes away. So Lizzie will go into the hospital.

If a heart becomes available to her—if there's a match, in other words—she will undergo a grueling operation that she may not survive. If she survives, she will endure the trials of postoperative recovery, of attempts by her own body to reject a foreign organ. Much can go wrong. Her body will become much more at risk to infections. But we have to try to trust, even though we realize someone else must die, probably a young person under tragic circumstances, for this to be attempted.

It is a miracle that Lizzie continues to do so well. But it is a miracle lived as if on an ice floe that, with spring now here, is melting imperceptibly, but melting nonetheless. Time is running out. If her life is to be meaningfully extended, then a transplant may well be God's miracle to accomplish that. It is a door through which we must try to go. We risk much, however, in going through it. Our lives will change still more. But through that door we must go.

Letter Twelve
May 20, 1996

LOOKING BACK
ON LETTER TWELVE

There is much evidence in the twelfth letter that I was wearing out. I would have denied this at the time, but I was wilting under the pressures.

I am one of those souls who thrives on having ten things going at once—at least, I used to think so. If I were not this way, I wouldn't have survived in the financial world. But battling Lizzie's cancer, as well as fighting for her transplant, I was consistently running ahead of problems as they arose. The problems I needed to deal with, such as fighting the insurance company's denial of a transplant, engaged every wit I could gather about me. I was becoming hypervigilant. I began to sleep like a young mother who always has an eye and an ear open for the cry of her sick baby. I was becoming an insomniac. I was irritable. After all the ground we'd bravely traveled, now I was falling apart. In the business world, I could often get my way if I thought enough, cared enough, used my contacts and money enough; if I planned well enough, if I used my influence. But in battling for Lizzie, and against her illnesses, I had met my match. No matter how much I planned, could spend, or could network to get her cared for and into the hands of the best doctors, it didn't seem to matter.

That powerlessness was unbearable.

I could see now why some people in crisis run away. Some turn to drugs or alcohol, or maybe take a lover. Such choices may not make their problems vanish, but at least, with each of these options, one creates an illusion that he's in control again, that he's doing *something,* that maybe he can, after all, choose the life he wants. Of course, it's a lie, and a particular kind of lie that never had any attraction for me during Lizzie's long illnesses. But I came to see how the lie could be attractive. In time, I sought and received professional help, and it helped. I never thought I was one who would need such help, but I'm grateful that I live in a time when my boundless anxieties and worries could be soothed, at least in part, by the fruits of medical wisdom.

Lizzie battled her own fears—often alone. That is Lizzie's coping style, seeking to save me more pain, even if her silence is more painful to me than her illnesses. When she received news that she could enter the hospital to be reconsidered for the transplant list, she realized she might never come home again. With only six hours' notice to move into the hospital indefinitely, she took Jonny out of his second-grade classroom to have lunch together at McDonald's. There, over a Happy Meal, she tried again to explain to a smart, but uncomprehending, eight-year-old her decision to try for a longer life by leaving him, Andrew, and me once more.

Lizzie wanted Jonny to enjoy a sense of security removed from the strange and scary medical underworld in which we now lived our lives, so he visited the hospital only once or twice a week. At the hospital, Jonny was, quite understandably, more taken by the 175 cable channels Mom got on her TV than he was by her. In fact, I doubt Jonny had even a clue as to how fragile his mom's life was. Smart as he was, as much as I tried to prepare him for what might be ahead, he could not comprehend that his mom might die, whatever dying means to an eight-year-old. His innocence of death was fine with Lizzie. And each time he left her, after his short visits, and her hospital room door closed behind him, her weakened heart broke again, as she struggled, over and over, often alone, wondering if this was the best way for our family to spend what could be her last days.

Lizzie told me only later that, in her loneliness at the hospital, she would try each evening to sit in her room's only chair facing west, over an interstate highway, to watch the sunset. Another day was passing. She knew she was a bit weaker, and there was no heart yet available. But there was a power she felt in the beauty of the sunsets that reminded her that the God of the universe, the same God who crafted each and every sunset, held the details of her life in His power. She didn't yet know what that might mean in her hope to extend her time with her family. She just had to trust. The sunsets and her hope gave her some peace amid the unfolding loneliness and desolation.

Lizzie remained forever hopeful, right up to the transplant. There were, of course, some moments when she succumbed to the stresses, but they were very few. In early May, with Lizzie, at the time, having been hospitalized for over two weeks, our insurance company called her and told her that they weren't going to pay for a transplant. She would have to go home, and, of course, that meant death.

"It wouldn't work," the insurance people said. "Besides, if you think your family can pay for the procedure and the follow-up care on your own, you don't realize that it will probably bankrupt you all." That brought her to tears, because it would hurt her family, and brought me, angrily, to track down the medical director at the insurance company and begin an appeal.

Then, just days later, one of the other patients awaiting a transplant got "his chance," as they say. Jeff would be the first person Lizzie would watch, from her hospital bed, go through the process. By then, she'd been living in her hospital room for a month. She was excited, hopeful—even a bit jealous, as were the others—to see Jeff get his chance at life.

But Jeff didn't make it.

Lizzie's and my naïve expectations that if she got this far, all she had to do was get through the surgery crashed and burned. We were brutally reminded that at the frontiers of medicine, people die. Lots of people. Lots of times. If death could come to Jeff and his family, after all he'd been through, I wondered whether this was the way we wanted to spend what might be our last days together.

A week or so later, another "waiter's" (that's what patients awaiting transplant are called) chance came. He didn't do well either, lingering between life and death for weeks after the surgery. The mood in the transplant suite darkened despite brave attempts at "hospital humor." One waiter had an empty beer bottle hung upside down from his IV pole, with plastic tubing coming down from the bottle. Another had a family of teddy bears. Lizzie, the gardener, rigged up her IV pole into an ivy pole, with plastic ivy and flowers for spring. With Memorial Day coming, she draped it with some flags.

Bravery and humor. We needed both, for Lizzie's time was running out.

Dear Friends,

So much has happened in the month since I last wrote. So much more probably lies ahead too. In our April 15th letter, we wrote of the hope we had that Lizzie might get on a transplant list. She entered the hospital on April 17 for an "evaluation"; and on April 22, she was officially placed on the national transplant registry.

Great news, huh? Now it's hard to know what to pray for. Can I pray that someone probably quite young would do something foolish soon and be killed in such a way (e.g., a massive head injury) that we can get a new heart for Lizzie? I confess that I struggle with such a prayer, yet the reality of what must happen is exactly that.

We are learning about yet one more subject (this time, organ transplantation) that neither of us had any plans to learn anything about, and wondering (at least I am), does this ever end?

Lizzie lives at the hospital awaiting a transplant. She has been there since April 17. If Lizzie were to go home, she would cease to be a "Status One" transplant candidate. With 20,000 hearts needed each year in the United States alone, and only 2,000 available, the difference between being a Status One and a Status Two is the difference, effectively, between getting a heart and not getting one. So here, too, Lizzie and I are fortunate. Waiting time for a heart, with Lizzie's blood type (A+), in this part of the country is estimated to be about two weeks to two months, with no guarantees that a heart will ever come; that Lizzie will live until, or through, the surgery; or that rejection, or infection, will not kill her in the post operative period. But the beautiful girl is doing fine so far. Since Lizzie has been in Fort Wayne's Lutheran Hospital, three heart transplants have been attempted; two have succeeded thus far. Lizzie and two others, both men (one with a different blood type from Lizzie's), await hearts, as well as about thirty other "Status Two" people who are at home with beepers.

We have also learned that Lizzie has been affected,

to some degree, by kidney damage. This is a new problem. Whether it is from the chemo or from the last six or seven months of low blood pressure, we do not yet know. It is possible that, with a new heart, the problem will be corrected. But it is just as likely, if not more likely, that the problem will survive the transplant and will have to be dealt with when normal blood pressure returns. The kidney problem could be (not "is") significant.

Lizzie also has been struck with gastrointestinal problems, which, it was initially feared, might be from a cancer recurrence, or a blockage. Wonderfully, that appears not to be the case after much testing. Rather, again, the problem appears to be the result of a poorly functioning heart. As with the kidneys, so too with the gastrointestinal problems, doctors tell us, "It's something we'll just have to watch after the transplant." Although Lizzie is many months out from her last chemo treatment, her white-blood-cell count is still low—not low enough to knock her off the transplant list, but low enough that it will pose an additional risk in the postoperative period when the real challenges begin. (We are told the transplant surgery per se *is not the hard part. Suppressing her immune system just enough to fight her own body's attempt to reject the new heart, yet not so much as to leave her lethally exposed to infections, is.) And of course, there are no guarantees that the breast cancer* will not return in yet another place in her body.

Facing all this does not grow easier with the passage of time. I find myself increasingly exhausted. Here we are at the threshold of transplantation, the point that seemed outlandish even to imagine a short time ago. But Lizzie, mentally, is through the whole transplant process, has recovered, and is out digging in her garden. (Indoors, however, she will have to give up her beloved birds, because of diseases they may carry that can kill people without functioning immune systems.)

I, on the other hand, feel as if we may be signing aboard a ride on the Challenger. Sweet Lizzie seems to know we've been aboard it all along. Her calm, her grace to everyone is legendary at the hospital. She and her sister Mary have decorated Lizzie's hospital room to look like an HGTV decorating makeover. (Now there's an angle for a new show—hospital room decoration!—yet to be exploited.) It's an oddly welcoming environment, befitting a beautiful person.

Prospects for a heart transplant have reenergized dear Lizzie, God bless her. (I'm not sure, though, that Lizzie was ever "unenergized.") It's just that I often do not know how she really feels. She hides much from me out of her own loving desire to shield me from the worst. So I wind up hearing bits and pieces of the "real story" from doctors, nurses, or other visitors. When I ask them how they find Lizzie, they tell me,

"Oh, she says she's fine, but she's worried about you."

I confess to bouts of emotional exhaustion a year and a half into this; to frequent sleeplessness, to lethargy, to distraction; and, with Lizzie's new symptoms emerging, I do not see where this ever ends. It goes on and on and on. Though I'm crazy about this woman, as long as I am on this side of Paradise, I'm affected by this roller-coaster life. I plead with God for a rest from new problems, for some kind of closure to the extent of the damage that has been done. But I see no closure. Layer by layer, it keeps unfolding, with potential new problems surfacing on top of old ones.

The apostle Paul tells me, "Three times I pleaded with the Lord to take it [his own 'thorn in the flesh'] away from me. But He said, 'My grace is sufficient for you, for my power is made perfect in weakness'" (2 Corinthians 12:8–9). I know, also, that Paul wasn't writing about failing to find a shirt in his size at Wal-Mart, but from the depths of his own long-term disappointment, confusion, and pain. And yes, I also know such moments, when the promise that "God will never leave us nor forsake us" (substantively, Hebrews 13:5), seems shallow. Or that "He will never give us a burden greater that we can handle" (substantively, 1 Corinthians 10:13) seems not to have considered this *trial.*

Yet I know, too, that "faith is being sure of what

we hope for and certain of what we do not see" (Hebrews 11:1). I do know that this is not for nothing, that God is not absent, and that this terrible trial for my sweet, dear, precious Lizzie serves a purpose—even if hidden—that is far bigger than I can grasp.

You all may well be part of this, in order that you may be deepened in your love and patience and concern for others. But I confess, it is not easy; and as time goes on—time that does not seem our friend—it does not get easier.

Please continue to keep us in your daily prayers.

Letter Thirteen
July 2, 1996

Looking Back
on Letter Thirteen

I'd been able to get to Lizzie's bedside every day during the two months prior to her transplant. Even then, as we accumulated staggering daily hospital bills for her care, we had not yet heard from our insurance company about our appeal. Despite my constant anxieties, on June 19 I took our middle son away to New England to look at colleges. Andrew was in his summer between junior and senior years in high school. On a beautiful Friday morning, June 21, I made what I thought would be a routine call back to Lizzie at about 11 A.M., eastern time, 10 A.M. in Indiana.

The day before, Lizzie was feeling down. I sensed one of the rare moments when I needed to play coach to Lizzie. She wondered that Thursday night when I called from New York state whether she would ever get a new heart. Lizzie had now been in the hospital, waiting, for just over two months. It was not just understandable impatience speaking. Lizzie was beginning to fail noticeably. Her kidneys were shutting down. Her gastrointestinal system was no longer working sufficiently. Just before leaving for New England, I had looked into the eyes of one of her doctors and asked what he thought of her deterioration. He said, "Lizzie needs a new heart." In those few words, he was telling me all I needed to know: Lizzie was, like all people awaiting a transplant, running out of time.

So when I heard her first words on the phone that Friday morning, I thought she was just trying to talk some courage into herself.

"Oh, Jimmy, I'm going to get a heart today."

"Good," I said. "That's the attitude. Be positive, Lizzie."

"No, Jimmy. Today's the day. I'm going to get a heart. They're doing tests right now on the donor."

I was speaking to Lizzie from a poorly lit, out-of-the-way corridor in the admissions office of Middlebury (Vermont) College. I started to cry. I was happy. I was terrified. I was angry that I was in Vermont, Lizzie was about to be strapped into a rocket, and I couldn't be there. I couldn't get there no matter how much I tried. Once again, I was upset with God that on this day of all days, maybe the last day of Lizzie's life, I was so far away. I cursed how unfair life was.

I needed a plan, a way to get back as quickly as possible.

I told Lizzie I would be there as soon as I could. I'd either drive or fly, but I'd be there as soon as I could. I'd call every hour on the hour until I heard from her that the transplant was a "go." Much testing still had to be done on the donor to see how good a match the heart was and how healthy it remained. The operation could still fall through at any minute. But I had to try to get back as quickly as I could. This would take hours, even if I started right away.

Andrew had remained out of earshot, in the admissions office waiting area. I wasn't sure he wanted to go home with me. His life, as a typically self-absorbed teenager, had suffered daily from the intrusions of his mom's endless illnesses over the past year and a half. The move to Indiana had been a special insult to him. I knew this college interview was important to him, if only for the illusion of normalcy it offered. It provided him welcome insulation from the chaotic conditions at home. I wanted to leave immediately, but I didn't want to deny Andrew his little window on normalcy these few days away seemed to provide. So I asked him to step outside with me. There, I told him what was up and asked what he wanted to do, including the possibility of taking me to the nearest airport. He gratified me by saying he wanted to go home right away. I was proud of him.

We went inside, and I told the admissions people at Middlebury that a family crisis demanded we leave immediately. By 11:30 A.M., we were on our way to White Plains Airport in New York, six hours away, with a hand-drawn sign in the back window saying "Medical Emergency." I was going to go as fast as I could drive. I called Lizzie every hour, on the hour. At 3 P.M., I found myself in the little town of Wassaic, New York There, I stopped in a bar, because it had a phone, and I made my call with no one around except the bartender, who was wiping his counter, getting ready to open.

Lizzie told me it was a "go." She was being prepped even as we spoke. She was joyful. She told me she had to go and would see me tomorrow. Things were going too fast for me. I was panicking.

"Wait! Wait! I love you." I felt myself trying to reach through the phone.

"I love you too," she told me. "I've got to go. 'Bye."

And that was all. We hung up. I fought back tears. The bartender was looking at me.

That may be our last conversation in this life, I thought. Yet at that moment, Lizzie had not, as was so often the case throughout her long, long illnesses, wanted to engage. Her way of coping was ever to put the best possible spin on events, no matter how dire. Always—in everything—be positive. Admit to no chink in the armor of hope.

Sometimes, I learned of new medical problems only by the arrival of new doctors' bills. I didn't always hear the news from Lizzie. My way was different. I, too, was hopeful. But I wanted, at least for that last second, to connect over the phone in the Wassaic bar and commemorate this solemn moment that might be our last one on earth. I wanted a moment to grieve what I might be about to lose forever.

When I finally got to the hospital at 10:30 P.M. that night, Lizzie was already out of a four-hour surgery. She waved her pinky at me. I was incredulous. And so grateful. To add to the joy, we'd heard that day that a fax had come from the insurance company authorizing the transplant.

But Letter Thirteen shows that the moment I arrived from Vermont and saw Lizzie had made it through the operation was the high point of the night. Things fell apart—badly—from there. What you don't read in Letter Thirteen is of a conversation I had over lunch the next day with our three boys, after a surgeon told us, "There is nothing more we can do." By noon on Saturday, June 22, with all three boys now at the hospital, the joy of last night had been replaced by the realization that we were witnessing, overnight and all morning, a slow fade to black: Lizzie's new heart, for some unknown reason, wasn't working. Alarms kept going off, which caused a flurry of activity in her suite. Family was ordered out. Curtains were closed. Again and again, they resuscitated her and brought her to higher and higher levels of life support. Everyone now knew she was going to die. We just didn't know when.

I wanted to break the news to the boys alone. I took them to a nearby Subway, hoping Lizzie would not die while we were out. Trying to control my emotions, I wanted them to know that the doctors had done their best, that their precious mom had done her best too. But, sometimes, even with all the skill we can muster and the best intentions, we don't get what we hope for. But as I was in agony forming each word and trying to be truthful but gentle, Jonny interrupted me, seeming to scold, "No, Dad, sometimes when a person gets a new heart, it just takes time for it to work."

Thinking I knew more than Jonny, and having been at the hospital from 5 A.M. watching Lizzie fail, I lowered my head, smiling faintly as my eyes teared up. "Yes, Jonny, maybe you're right."

In the month that followed, Lizzie would be back in the hospital, suffering from cardiac rejection. Days after the transplant, her immune system tried to kill her new heart—again—seeing it as a foreign object in her body. Then, three weeks after the transplant, she was under the surgeon's knife for another suspicious lump, this time in her other breast—a possible recurrence of cancer. That lump proved, mercifully, to be benign. But by then, we were both crazy from the stresses of what we kept going through. We had no reservoirs of energy left, and yet we were being asked to tackle more challenges.

God, where are You? I wondered. Were we again sitting on a curb, spent and collapsed, about to be told to run yet another marathon?

Dear Friends,

Lizzie has received a heart transplant!
Some of you already may have heard that Lizzie
was transplanted on Friday, June 21. She received the heart of a twenty-one year-old woman
from southern Indiana, in a surgery that was
textbook perfect.

I was in Vermont looking at colleges with
Andrew when, at 11 A.M., I made what I
thought would be a routine call to the hospital to
see how sweet Lizzie was doing. Andrew was
about to go into an interview at Middlebury.
But with our news on Lizzie, we left immediately, getting back to Ft. Wayne at 10:30 P.M.

Lizzie was just out of surgery, in intensive care, but able—remarkably able, I thought—to respond to commands, nod, wave weakly, and make eye contact that seemed to say, "Isn't this something?" The surgeon told me all was going amazingly well and suggested I go home and catch some sleep. This would be a long process, and he assured me the easy part, the "mechanical part"—was over. The hard part, the "cerebral part," was now ahead.

At 4:30 A.M., the surgeon, still attending sweet Lizzie, woke me at home to tell me things were not going well. Perhaps I might want to come up. No need to rush. He was on top of things and doing what could be done, but Lizzie was slipping.

Unfortunately, the next twelve hours did not go any better. Lizzie deteriorated rapidly, with doctors unable to stabilize basic heart functions as they brought her to successively higher levels of advanced life support. At 10:30 A.M., on Saturday morning, June 22, we lost her briefly. One of the heart surgeons, at that moment performing another operation, left his patient to return to Lizzie. He successfully resuscitated her. Then, he took me aside and told me, "If she slips through again, there's nothing more we can do. I'm sorry. Sometimes, even when we think everything looked so good, it just doesn't work out." And then he went back to the operating room.

We who clung to Lizzie at her bedside were left

alone to ponder what we had just heard. I cried. Lizzie's mother handled the latest news more stoically. I prayed, too. We were assured Lizzie was not in pain. Her vital signs began to deteriorate once again before noon, but miraculously, she began to stabilize and remained stable for the next twenty-four hours, showing increased strength and health in her heart's function during the days that immediately followed.

However, in a couple of days, her kidneys began to fail, one of the possibilities we had been alerted to before transplantation. Once again, we could only sit back, watch, and pray as specialists tried to assess whether the kidney problem was temporary or permanent. Only time will tell for sure, but as of today, the problem seems to be temporary, thank God.

The press has done several stories on Lizzie, and bits of them wound up going national. (See them on www.lettersforlizzie.com.) I hoped that the stories could prove helpful if we needed to battle the insurance company further. However, the insurance company came through on the very day of her transplant, not knowing a donor heart had just become available to Lizzie.

It's likely Lizzie will come home this week. We are grateful people for all that has happened, even if saddened that this miraculous turn has come about, in part, at the expense of a twenty-one-year-old and her family.

I wish we could say that Lizzie and I are now looking at each other over an iced tea on our porch, saying, "Whew, I'm glad that's over. What do you want to do now?" But we have no such luxury. We have been given, by God and medical science—and the life of an unfortunate, unnamed young woman —the gift of some more time.

How much? We don't know. For what purpose? That, too, remains to be discovered. But we hope we may be a blessing to many who struggle with some of the same issues sweet Lizzie has been struggling with so heroically over the past eighteen months. We thank God for this gift, for the time, for the vision we have been given. And we thank you, dear people, for your faithful friendship and prayers thus far.

As I wrote about a year ago, and now write again, I hope this is our last letter on Lizzie's frightful health for a long, long time.

EIGHT YEARS LATER:
Some Afterthoughts

By the end of July 1996, having battled terminal cancer and end-stage heart failure, Lizzie and I mopped our brows and, to make an analogy, sat exhausted on a beach where once our home had stood. A huge storm had blown it away. Hardly a trace of it remained. Hurt, dripping wet, and stunned, we sat taking in the calm that had returned.

The sun peeked out from the clouds. A smidgen of blue sky framed the setting sun. Giving every ounce of strength we had and clutching at the smallest morsels of God's grace, we had survived a Category Five hurricane, just barely. We wondered what might be ahead. A tornado? Why not? It had happened before. We felt defenseless and beaten. But we were still alive.

Eight years have now passed. My sweet Lizzie is still by my side, thank God. Our children have had the gift of their loving mother for eight more years. We celebrated our thirty-second wedding anniversary in August 2003. But therapies and medicines undertaken to save Lizzie's life have had their own hellish way with her. Lizzie has suffered heart attacks, stomach problems, low blood pressure, blood disorders, shingles, double pneumonia, and the persistent rejection of her new heart by her own ingenious immune system. And her kidneys have failed. We have had to begin investigating the wisdom of finding a kidney transplant. We have again faced death —more than once. But Lizzie is still alive, thank God.

If Lizzie's most acute health problems seemed to end after the heart transplant, by July 1996 chronic problems began to appear and have only seemed to grow. My own problems with anxiety and vigilance also persisted and grew. That there was no longer any obvious enemy in my beloved Lizzie to battle against did not shake my fear that another one was just ahead. As my anxiety grew, my sleeplessness increased. I even came to fight more often with Lizzie as I (as well as she, poor girl) struggled to adjust to the many medicines and side effects that we both had to negotiate.

Our coping skills, too, differed so much that at times they became a source of conflict. Often—too often, perhaps—I wanted to talk about what we'd been through. I needed to process, out loud, some of what had happened. But this was not helpful to Lizzie, who kept telling me, "These are the good times, Jimmy. Everything's fine."

To me, though, things weren't fine. And might never again be fine. Any day, I suspected, the rain might start again and the winds pick up.

In our culture, we want to put horrid experiences behind us, try to forget about them, get over them. I have become one who has seen horrible suffering, much of it pointless, without redeeming value, as far as I can see. I don't think I will ever "get over it," though I have come to process its aftereffects better; and I have learned to keep its darkest images from many who, I sense, do not—and cannot—understand because they have not been similarly tested. I do not wish others to suffer because I have, but I wish other people—especially Christians—had a greater capacity to walk a bit further alongside that under-class of chronically ill sufferers and their caregivers for whom closure doesn't seem to exist.

Our experience tells me that even Christians burn out from caregiving. They are great in the opening moments, bringing a meal and cleaning up, which are tremendous blessings. But as the days of illness turn into weeks and months and even years, they fall away, understandably, to get back to their own lives. Worse still is the sense I felt from some Christians who felt that, because our problems were not relieved by their prayers, maybe Lizzie and I had some unconfessed sin or some special reason to be singled out by God to be stretched on the rack.

Faith, character, and attitude in the sufferer and in the care-giver matter increasingly as time goes on—because as time goes on we fight on alone. The suffering even intensifies as we become invisible, as we are no longer heard. We see a veil come down before our physicians', nurses', friends', and fam-ilies' eyes as they see a sick person as incurable. The sufferer is abandoned, unknowingly and unintentionally, by many who just can't take it; they don't want to believe that such awful things can happen to them or their loved ones because, if they think too deeply or too long about it, they realize the devastation could happen to them.

Yes, faith and character and attitude matter. Our will and our choices are critical. But we are still human, made of flesh and blood. If cut, we still bleed. We hurt. We are not statues in a spiritual museum.

But once through that horrible first July, during which Lizzie had to go back to surgery for the removal of another suspicious breast lump, things did begin to settle down. Finally. Lizzie did remarkably well. True, we regularly had, and still have, to go to the hospital for a variety of matters, and Lizzie's body has been subjected to the ravages of a host of ailments that probably would not touch someone who's not immuno-compromised or taking the medicines she must take. Yet we have been fortunate. Lizzie has done so well over the eight years since her heart transplant, more than nine since she was first treated for cancer. Despite all the trouble, we are among the blessed. We have each other. We have life. We still have faith. And hope, again, for the time we have left together.

Yet having now shared the worst of our journey, might there be some lessons, or reflections, to pass on from the bru-tal classrooms of Lizzie's illnesses? Might there be afterthoughts that could help others struggling, not only with life-threatening illness, but with any of the awful circumstances life can pre-sent? Perhaps there are a few lessons our story has to offer. Looking back from nine years out, we would be crazy to have chosen any of it, but there was, and is, good that has come out of it.

Like what?

Perhaps a story might help explain.

I like to read. I like to read challenging things that make me think and help me understand life and the world around me. I read lots of theology, history, and philosophy. The way I see it, if you or I have, say, to play a game, we should understand the rules of the game as well as we possibly can. While life is no game, I believe there are rules that govern how to live life well. Maybe the suffering Lizzie and I have endured has increased my desire to understand more, to learn from what we were enduring, to search out lessons, to help make sense of so much suffering.

Why, nine years ago, so soon after coming to Huntington to serve our God more intentionally by teaching at a Christian college and giving up high-paying work, would my sweet Lizzie have become so ill? I know, in this life, there is no answer, but I am one who asks such questions and turns them over in his mind. Had I missed something in coming? Should I not have come? Was there some disobedience that I had committed that brought on Lizzie's suffering? I know throughout history people have suffered horribly—far worse than we have. And Christians are not exempt from suffering. Perhaps they are even especially called to suffer, as was Jesus Himself.

Did John the Baptist receive just punishment for abandoning his own ministry as Jesus' ministry grew? Did he suffer from some unconfessed sin that led to his beheading after having baptized Jesus? I don't think so. John was one of God's most faithful. But John's faithfulness did not exempt him from inexplicable suffering.

Lizzie's and my suffering, too, seemed senseless. But that did not stop me from trying to understand what its purpose might be. Because, in some way, I assumed it must have a purpose.

I read lots. Scripture has been important, as it always is for me, especially the book of Job and commentaries on it. These were among my favorites, as were, to pick just two others, C.S. Lewis's *A Grief Observed* and Sheldon Vanauken's *A Severe Mercy*.

But there was another story, a historical account of an event I'd first read back in college. That's over thirty years ago, but that tale came alive for me only in the dark days of 1995 and 1996, when I sorely needed inspiration to courage and duty. Herodotus, the Greek historian, had recorded the story over two thousand years ago. Leonidas, the Spartan general, was the subject. Leonidas had tried to hold a mountain pass at Thermopylae in northern Greece in August 480 B.C., against vastly superior forces of Persian King Xerxes. Herodotus tells us the Persians had three million soldiers. That number's outlandish. But the Persians had far more men than the Greeks, who probably had little more than six thousand soldiers gathered from a loose confederation of Greek city-states. Worse still, after Leonidas had sent many of his men away to safer ground, probably no more than one thousand were left in place at Thermopylae to defend the pass through which the

Persians would come on their journey south to conquer the Greek peninsula below Thermopylae.

Amazingly, Leonidas and his band of one thousand held the pass for three days, as much from grit and courage as from the Persians' inability to get more than a couple of hundred men at any one time into the narrow pass to wage war. But in time a Greek traitor showed the Persians a way around the pass; and as dawn broke on the final day of battle, Leonidas and his men awakened to find themselves surrounded and trapped by a Persian horde grown more angry and vengeful by the frustration the Greeks had caused them. Of course, Leonidas was the special object of the Persians' wrath. And the Persians killed him and every one but two of his men. Leonidas may have tried, and perhaps succeeded, to send a messenger back to Sparta before the end came. We're not sure, but Herodotus tells us that at the sight of the Thermopylae massacre, the Greeks erected a tribute to the fallen with the words Leonidas may have tried to get back to Sparta: "Passerby, tell the Spartans that we behaved as they hoped we would."

In the end, Persia would not win their war against Greece, though for a while, after Thermopylae, they would control the central part of the country. Within months, at the battle of Salamis, the entire Persian army would be driven off the Greek peninsula. The united Greeks at Salamis might later claim that part of their inspiration to overcome a vastly superior Persian force had come from Leonidas and his message. And 2,500 years later, Leonidas' message aroused courage and hope in me that, no matter what happened to my dear Lizzie, with God's help we, too, might send forth the same message:

"Passerby, tell anyone who's interested that we behaved as they hoped we would."

Lizzie and I live in a time when a sharp divide separates belief and behavior. In fact, our beliefs are often more evidenced by the choices we make and the deeds we perform than by the words we utter. Big names from politics, from the entertainment world, even from religious life confront us with painful examples of those who have believed one thing and done another. They have shamed themselves and, in some cases, the causes they upheld or the people who looked up to them.

Illness and adversity—like battle's heat—are never sought, if one is sane. But if they come our way, few circumstances better define the character of human beings.

Lizzie and I didn't enter our Thermopylae with proven characters. We surely hoped, as all decent people do, that if adversity ever struck, we would stand firmly. But, in truth, we didn't know how we would behave. It's not the same as driving west across Montana in a blizzard and thanking your lucky stars once you reach Spokane that the danger is over. Our journey is not yet finished, even now—and may well, in time, take us into even greater treacheries. But we've journeyed thus far trying to keep in mind the connection between what we claim to believe and how we ought to behave.

Nevertheless, we are far enough now to offer some observations from our own fierce fight at Thermopylae to any who care to hear or might have ears to listen. We offer these observations on our experiences in the hope that they will prove helpful to those who find themselves, one day, ambushed in their own Valley of the Shadow of Death. We know many have suffered and will suffer more grievously than Lizzie and I, so we don't mean to offer the final word on suffering. These are, rather, personal observations, not biblical truths. We hope, however, that our insights may offer hope, comfort and encouragement, and, perhaps, a godly path through the trials in which life can ensnare us or our loved ones, if we live long enough.

UNDERSTAND WHAT YOU NEED.

"Rugged individualism" will almost certainly lead you to overestimate how much you can accomplish yourself and underestimate what help others might be. "Thanks, but we're fine" is a noble—but foolish—statement when the Persians surround your Thermopylae. The sense of abandonment is real in advanced illness, both to the patient and to the caregiver. Such a time is hardly the moment to stand alone and tough it out—but many try to. Lizzie and I desperately needed hope. While medicine didn't always offer that hope, the community of friends surrounding us did. Many times, at critical points of despair or loss, God seemed remote, but we felt His touch constantly through dear people who came alongside us and upheld us at those moments.

Don't isolate yourself from those who want to help. You will need them.

ACCEPT THE LOVE OF THOSE WHO CAN GIVE IT, AND
UNDERSTAND THAT SOME WILL NEVER UNDERSTAND.

Not everyone can enter into your suffering with you. Some
who can, and do, will not enter in the way you might have
wished, the way you think would be most helpful and comforting. Others just don't have the gift of words or the courage
to speak them. They may change your oil or bring a cake and
then vanish. Still others will say dumb things. In our case,
what I found the most hurtful—of course, knowing they meant
no hurt—were our friends who said nothing at all.

You will find something of a rearrangement of your
friends and acquaintances. Some who you might have thought
would have drawn close in a horrible time will surprise and
hurt you by retreating, and others, from whom you may have
expected nothing, will astound you in their courage and faithfulness. Don't fixate on the disappointments; celebrate the
gifts, whatever they are.

LEARN ALL YOU CAN WITHOUT OBSESSING.

Serious, life-threatening illness is not like fighting a cold.
You don't need "attitude" to beat most colds. But you need
attitude to fight life-threatening battles. A good attitude will
not save a desperately ill person, and a bad attitude will not
condemn one, either. But if you or a loved one ever face the
worst, a great attitude won't hurt. In fact, looking back, there
were two attitudes, as I noted in Letter Four, that seemed to

separate those who did well from the many who didn't.

First, the survivors seemed to learn everything possible about their condition so that they were able, along the way and as appropriate, to make informed decisions about the care (or lack of care) they wanted to receive. Second, they understood that they would never understand it all. It's a hard balance: Learn everything you can, but don't obsess. You're not going to get all your questions answered, no matter how important they seem. Prayer here, for me, was important. Doctors might not have the time or interest to listen to my questions; my friends, many times, didn't have the experience. But God would be there to help me center, focus, or calm down.

If prayers wore shoes, mine wore out carpets in several places. Here are several of my favorite prayers, all short—short enough to be easily memorized and prayed day or night over and over again:

"Lord, give me the courage to change the things that I can, the patience to accept the things that I can't, and the wisdom to know the difference."

John 14:27: *"Do not let your hearts be troubled and do not be afraid."*

Teresa of Avila's little gem: *"Let nothing bother you; let nothing frighten you. All things pass. Patience gains all. God alone is enough."*

And the beautiful words of Juliana of Norwich, which she claimed Jesus told her at a time of extreme illness: *"All will be well, and all will be well, and all manner of things will be well."*

FORGET ABOUT TIME AND ANSWERS, YET VALUE THE TIME AND ANSWERS YOU HAVE.

When serious illness strikes, we are awakened from our foggy sleep in which there once was all the time in the world. Tragedy reminds us, brutally, that we don't have time, and that the time we have may not always be our friend. Life is a gift, and that gift is made up of time. For Lizzie and me, more time became the goal. We realized, early on, that Lizzie had been hit so hard and so much that she quite likely was not going to get her "three score and ten." But we were not going to surrender easily; we were going to get as much time as we could possibly get. Like ballplayers in extra innings, we just wanted to keep the rally going—or at least keep the opposition from scoring any more runs.

Serious illness acquaints one with a new kind of time too: medical time. Medical time is like no other time in the world. Like the sign Dante envisioned over the gates of Hell in his *Divine Comedy,* "All hope abandon, ye who enter here," so too you may despair of time upon entering the offices of any specialty physician's waiting room or medical facility, but especially those "elites" who are good at what they do and practice something that doesn't offer enough of them to go around to all who need them. So get used to waiting.

And waiting.

And waiting some more.

I've known families of patients who went crazy from the uncertainty—and from the waiting. They don't realize that their loved one's doctors are trying to get to them as soon as they can, are working at the frontiers of medical knowledge, and may not themselves know what, if anything, will work. But the best of doctors keep trying to "work the problem."

Live as normally as possible.

If you are caught in a siege, say, fighting the Persians at Thermopylae, try to live your life as normally as possible. If you go to a stamp-collecting club on Thursdays, keep going. If you go to church or enjoy a weekly conversation with your mechanic at the gas station or like to have your hair done on Wednesdays, keep doing these things. They are good counterpoints to the madness that is often on the verge of overwhelming your life.

Lizzie let all her gardening and home-decorating magazine subscriptions—activities she dearly loved—lapse. This concerned me because it was a chink in the armor of hope. She also wanted to move her dresser out of our bedroom. I protested strongly. Hope is the "currency of the realm" when disaster strikes.

Someone condemned to death under Henry VIII was asked his final wish and said, improbably, that he would like time to teach the king's horse to talk; and he thought he'd need about a year to do it. Well, his accusers were flabbergasted but went along with the outlandish request, probably for no other reason than just to see what would happen. Visitors and friends who came to his cell expressed amazement that he had made such a foolish request, but the condemned knew exactly what he was doing. "Look," he told them, "three things can happen in the next year. The king may die. I may die. Or the horse may learn to talk."

And for anyone else in a seemingly hopeless situation, he or she must continue to hold out hope that the Persians won't get through the pass, that things will change, that a miracle will happen, that, just maybe, a horse may learn to talk.

In the meantime, live as normally as possible. Even if you feel it is a lie.

BUILD A SUPPORT NETWORK, EVEN
IF FOR THE FIRST TIME IN YOUR LIFE.

With Lizzie so sick, I was surprised how much I needed people—how much *both of us* needed people—to share the burdens of the day. I remember speaking to one woman on the phone who said she wanted to do something. I told her to pray for us. She wanted to do more. She said she had already been praying for us. She said she wanted to do something tangible. I didn't know what to say.

I recall one day walking into one of our upstairs bathrooms and being surprised to find two dear women in the same room.

One was on her knees in the bathtub, looking up, smiling at me, scrubbing away. We already had people doing so many things for us that there was not a lot left for me to do except take what care I could of Lizzie and talk to as many people as I could who wanted to do something for us. But it is important to try to give the supporting community a chance to serve. Their work is a gift to the sufferer. But your ability and willingness to let them serve is a loving gift to them as well.

Oddly, as I've tried to help others who have been walloped by family disasters I've learned that my own reaction was different from many. Much to my surprise, some of the people who reached out to help us more than eight years ago have since undergone their own trials. When I've offered to help, or just to talk, they've responded, "Oh, everything's fine. Thanks anyway. We'll get back to you."

Suffering itself is hard. But it leaves us vulnerable to depression, anxiety, and other bad stuff as a result of isolation and alienation. So, if you're in the "deep yogurt" of suffering, don't try to go it alone. Don't believe for one minute your hurting neighbor or loved one who says, after the devastating diagnosis, "Oh, I'm fine. Really!" They may not know what to say. They may feel they would be embarrassed if they were to lose their composure. They may wonder if they are worth anyone else's care or trouble. But they are not "fine." Inside, they are broken-down messes. They need your love. And patience. They need your reaching out. They need community badly, even if they tell you to go away.

APPRECIATE THE GRACE GIVEN.

Many who know me would assume I have deep faith, but I still struggled with appreciating the grace, as given, along the way. For those who may not know what I mean by grace, let me say that I'm using the term theologically here, not culturally. By "grace," I mean the "unmerited favor, or gift, of God," not the cultural sense of winsomeness or attractiveness.

In many ways and at many times in our struggles, I pounded, and kept pounding, on the gates of heaven for God to intervene to save my Lizzie's life. Whether one believes God caused her illnesses or allowed them is for me far less important than that in the middle of the worst of it I pleaded for relief and often found none to be had. I pleaded, in truth, not just for relief, but for specific kinds of relief—that a test would come back a certain way, that surgery would not be necessary, that a certain drug would work. But I failed—and sometimes failed badly—to cut God some slack in the way in which He would send His grace.

At times, you see, I became like a little child on the living room floor, crying so hard that I refused to open my eyes to see any loving soul offering me a toy. And when, at long last, I did open my eyes, I grabbed the toy, red-faced, tears streaming down my cheeks, teeth clenched, only to fling it against the wall—because God would not give me what *I* wanted.

I carried on with God that way quite often and over a long time. I remember once being almost alone at Lutheran Hospital, lost in anger and self-pity, and only after many minutes did I realize there was a skylight in the lovely waiting room in which I was seated, and that sunlight was streaming through it, playing on various objects in the room, filtering dust particles, dancing on walls, murals, and chairs.

No, it was not what I wanted. What I wanted was Lizzie to be all better, and I wanted the madness that kept unfolding in our lives to stop. I wanted to go back to the time before Lizzie was ever sick. But those skylights and the sunlight dancing on the waiting room walls at Lutheran Hospital were little gifts of beauty and peace.

The light's fall and the room's peace did give *an* answer—maybe not *the* answer I wanted—but a little answer from God, nonetheless. He was still there. He was with me. And He offered a little gift, like the toy offered to the crying child on the living room floor, to try to tide me over for a little while longer. I'm sure I missed many other gifts He sent me along the battle-front Lizzie and I had to travel, but I'm grateful I didn't completely miss the light's fall that day.

LEARN WHAT'S IMPORTANT AND WHAT'S NOT.

Like little else can, illness and tragedy move our focus off the frivolous.

I would never wish on my worst enemy what Lizzie and I have endured. But strangely, there were and are unmistakable benefits from our sufferings, as there are for many who remain open to what tragedy can teach us. In a way, there might even be blessings. Among the most significant of those blessings is our growing sense of what is truly important in life.

Even though at some level we know better, many of us get caught up in how we look, being a little overweight, what the rude guy at the checkout line meant by a flippant remark, how our lawn looks, or what to wear to our next party. When disaster strikes, a powerful magnet sweeps over our lives and lifts away all the minor metal that clings to us, leaving only the heavy gold, silver, and platinum.

The Spanish have a proverb: "A shroud has no pockets." I've also heard that no one ever saw a U-Haul at a funeral. In the end, *things* matter little, but the quality and depth of our relationships matter deeply. Here, I urge you—no, plead with you—before the darkest hours of life come: Be reconciled to those you love and who love you. Above all, be reconciled with your Creator God. If you have had good relationships with those closest to you, those relationships will probably withstand the blows of suffering. They might even grow deeper. But if respect and thoughtfulness were in short supply before things went bad, the stresses of tragedy may strain these fragile bonds past their breaking point.

GIVE IT YOUR BEST SHOT, EVEN IF THE ODDS ARE AGAINST YOU.

Lizzie and I made the acquaintance of many courageous ill people along our way. At different times, these heroes cheered us on; at other times, we cheered them on. Along our way, we met many whose illnesses did not seem as deadly as others', yet they died. Other times, we met seemingly hopeless cases —as Lizzie's appeared to be—but the patient lived. The strong ones didn't always make it, despite their courage and determination. But a remarkable group of those supposedly hopeless cases lived longer than anyone thought at first.

There are no guarantees in life other than, in the end, we will all die. And there are especially few guarantees along the frontiers of major, life-threatening illness. Few people get to look over the ledge we have looked over, the one that separates life from death, and come back to talk about it. We know we are among the very, very few who have returned—at least for a while—to tell of that harrowing experience.

If you ever have to look over that ledge, don't faint. Don't wither amid the strain. Dylan Thomas's poem "Do Not Go Gentle into That Good Night" puts the truth about our respect for the life God has lent us in its proper light. Yes, "There is a time for everything . . . a time to live and a time to die," Ecclesiastes tells us. And I'm sure that when the time finally comes to stand face-to-face with the Lord, it will be a great day. But I would urge those battling to hold on to the gift of life they have received as they raise a young child, as Lizzie so wanted to, to fight with everything God gives them the means to fight with.

You can expect to be paralyzed by shock and fear when the deadly diagnosis is first made. That's normal. But get beyond that. Fight. God has given you the gift of life. Don't give it up easily. Don't claim graceful acceptance before you have truly exhausted the wondrous, God-given gifts of medicine to fight. Don't hide cowardice behind grace. God's grace will accompany you every step of the way. But fight to live, to bless others, to have more time with your family, and to help this broken and needy world.

If a clinical trial is your best hope, try it. If a new medicine, go for it. But don't just give up. You may, of course, have to surrender in time. But don't freeze in fear, like a deer in the headlights of an oncoming truck, after the initial diagnosis.

TRUST GOD.

In spite of everything, keep trusting God. But how different trust becomes on the battlefield when real guns have you in their crosshairs, as Lizzie has known throughout her harrowing experience. Before Lizzie's illnesses, we had known sufferings, yes. We had fought through my own dissatisfactions with marriage. We had struggled with serious parenting challenges that left us heartsick and discouraged. But somehow these earlier eruptions in our lives did not disconnect me from the grand illusion that I was in control of my life. And it was, I think, through those earlier painful times that God broke through my own walls of unbelief and arrogance to break me and change my heart.

Therefore, when mighty illnesses struck Lizzie, I thought that I knew God; that I had Him in a box, so to speak; that I knew how He operated and what He valued most. I thought He valued *my* happiness and *my* contentment, since I was pledged to Him, more than anything else. I assumed that He would protect me always, in ways I would understand, since I had sacrificed the comforts and familiarity of my East Coast life and ventured out to serve Him in Huntington, Indiana.

But in truth, I don't think when the suffering began that I had a clue about God. Only our family's devastation began to introduce me to Him in a way I could never have imagined. I found God loving, yes, but very challenging—more interested in my character and my soul's growth than I ever would have thought. In C. S. Lewis's *The Lion, the Witch, and the Wardrobe*, Mr. and Mrs. Beaver are asked about Aslan, the great lion who serves as an image of Jesus in the story. The children in the story ask, "Is he—quite safe?" Mr. Beaver replies, "Who said anything about safe? 'Course he isn't safe. But he's good."

God's love for me, for any of us, isn't always safe. In fact, God is little interested in our mere safety. Or our happiness. Or our comfort, for that matter. He wants us to become changed beings, not followers of rituals, not consumers of a religion chasing earthly happiness and material pleasures. He wants us to become wholly "new creations."

Still, there are strange, dark expanses of His love that I can't explain even today, depths that only mystery and faith can plumb. A remark comes to mind from another C. S. Lewis classic, *The Screwtape Letters*, in which a senior devil instructs a young devil in the ways of corrupting human beings. At one point, in Letter VIII, the senior devil writes, "Our cause is never more in danger than when a human, no longer desiring, but still intending, to do our Enemy's will, looks round upon a universe from which every trace of Him seems to have vanished, and asks why he has been forsaken, and still obeys."

I want to obey, and trust, too, even when there is seemingly nothing to gain.

I've just begun to understand this God who is far richer and more complex than the cosmic Santa Claus I used to think was at my beck and call. The Master Creator, unimaginably, wants to partner with little me in redeeming His world—but only on His terms, terms that quite often are different from mine.

Yes, I've grown in my trust of God; I understand a little better what that trust means. But still, after all Lizzie and I have been through, I don't trust very well.

I also wrestle with those faithful souls who are quick to speak for God, who purport to know God's will. These souls speak always, I know, to bless, never to harm. Yet somehow they are sure things will turn out fine. Or, if not, it will be best that God take Lizzie home to be with Him.

They may be right. At one time I might have said the same kind of things to others. But I've learned to be careful about saying such things to people who are in the midst of deep suffering. People struggling at such moments are especially fragile, and, if they're honest, their faith is fragile too. Those with pat answers can, without meaning to, seem callous, presenting an image of a God who doesn't seem to listen to their pleadings or isn't able to help them. God doesn't need people to defend His honor or interpret His mysteries when the bereaved rage.

Better it may be for most of us to say nothing at such times. Just sit with the afflicted or the grieving. Be their friend, not necessarily the one to provide answers to questions that have stumped the brightest minds for centuries. Just be there to listen.

More important, God will be there. We can't always know how, but He's there. Perhaps in no other way than were those who knelt at the foot of His Son's cross and wept for their Friend and His family.

We won't have all our questions answered in this world. Days turn into weeks, weeks into months, months into years. Lizzie and I have passed the nine-year mark in fighting her illnesses. In the years after a seeming victory over cancer, as we run with all we've got for more time, heart problems entered the race, as have, more recently, kidney, lung, and stomach problems. As time has passed it has not gotten easier; if anything, we now have less energy to fight with. Compared to the opening weeks and months of the fight against cancer in the early days of 1995, when we were filled with vigor and resolve, today we are injured, tired, and malnourished in facing the continuing race to stay ahead of Lizzie's next setback.

But that has made our fight all the more God's and less our own. We don't have what it takes. We will either get the grace from God for today or we won't go on. Friends who, once upon a time, closely tracked our daily trials no longer keep up with us. They have, understandably, returned to the rhythms of their own lives. We're not upset by that. We're realists. We're grateful for what each and every one of them gave us, when they did, but respect their need to give their vital energies to their own lives and families.

Yes, it's hard. But it also, in some ways, has gotten easier. For too long, I think, I expected a miracle of a particular sort. That was dangerous. Since then, we have learned to live better with the uncertainty, or maybe have learned to live with it as another strange gift we have received along the way. Our fight is a different kind of battle from those who lose a loved one some morning after coffee and kisses around the breakfast table, who then go off and die in a crash at seventy miles an hour. There, closure is swift and brutal. With us, closure is elusive. We simply drift down, like people falling off a cliff in slow motion.

Or perhaps, to take up again the analogy of Letter Seven that touched us deeply in the late summer of 1995, after Lizzie had been diagnosed with end-stage heart failure, we are like the crew of Apollo 13. But in our case we don't get to come home; at least, not to the home we once knew. We just drift farther and farther out into space, watching the darkness deepen, the dials trim lower, the systems fail, slowly, relentlessly. Yes, we still have each other on the journey so far. Yes, we also have the grace of a God who has loved us and ridden beside us all the way. But we will not make it back to what was once home, as the Apollo 13 astronauts did once they hit the blue Pacific and were taken aboard a raft.

Our journey is different. Different for reasons we probably won't ever fully understand. God has given Lizzie nine more years since the cancer diagnosis; and with each passing month, and the eruption of each new crisis, we are amazed that we've gotten this far—a long way from the conversation

Lizzie and I once had in Stan Rich's office in fall 1995, while we awaited his arrival. Then Lizzie hoped God would give her twelve more years, just twelve—until Jonny would be eighteen, probably heading off to college and, for Lizzie, able to stand on his own.

Jonny is now sixteen. He's had the wonderful good fortune to have his mom for nine years longer than he might have. Sweet Lizzie has seen our oldest son, Nick, graduate from college and marry; and she's gotten to see our middle son, Andrew, graduate from college and start his career. But having gotten all the time we've gotten has only made us want more.

My love and admiration for this brave, good woman has only grown and matured as her illnesses have robbed her more and more of energy, charm, and superficial attractiveness. Seeing Lizzie's slowly declining capacities to work, to walk, to travel remind me that we are still living on a bubble. Her precious life can end at any time.

In truth, I think we live the kind of lives God would want us all to live:

Lives that don't know about tomorrow.

Lives ever grateful for today and eager to make our todays all God would want us to make of them.

Lives ever certain that our days are in His hands.

January 1995: When Lizzie was diagnosed with cancer, a group of new Indiana friends made this "Friendship Quilt."

Fall 1988: Lizzie with our youngest, Jonny, born in March.

January 1996: Lizzie's heart failed as a result of the cancer treatments. Friends Jeannie (left) and Mimi flew in to say good-bye.

Same day: Middle son Andrew, then 17; Jim; and Mary, Lizzie's youngest sister, who had come from New Mexico to help.

In spite of "chemo hair," IVs and constant weakness, Lizzie kept trying—for everyone else.

March 1996: Lizzie was sent home on February 5 to die. On March 8, Jonny turned 8, and his mom was alive and ready to celebrate.

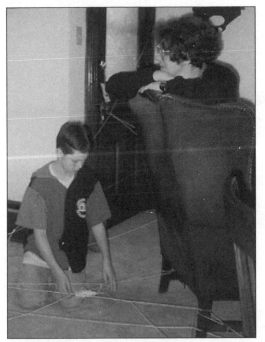

Our kids loved to play a game of "spider web" at their birthdays when they were young. This time the game was set up by Lizzie's sister Ann, but Lizzie didn't want to miss the fun.

April 1996: We had been told in the past that Lizzie was not a suitable candidate for a heart transplant. But on this spring day we headed off to the hospital for a three-day evaluation—with no promises.

June 1996: post transplant: Lizzie's mom, Carol, and I check in on our heroine.

June 1996: The week before Lizzie's transplant, Mary and Jonny came for a visit. Lizzie kept presents tucked away to keep him coming back.

May 1996: With Lizzie weakening in the hospital while awaiting a new heart, our oldest son Nick drove ten hours in a borrowed car to see her.

ACKNOWLEDGMENTS

A first book is always an act of faith for any who support it. *Letters for Lizzie* is no exception. Without the kindness and support of my friend Ken Swanson, this work may never have seen the light of day. Thank you, Ken.

Through Ken I was introduced to my literary agent John Eames, who tirelessly sought a publisher for *Letters for Lizzie* and, all the while, encouraged me to write more. Thank you, John.

John found Moody Publishers, where I was introduced to Mark Tobey, who believed in this book enough to see that it would be published. Thank you, Mark.

In turn, Mark put the book into the hands of a talented and challenging editor, Betsey Newenhuyse, whose deft yet gentle touch has only enhanced whatever chance this book might have to touch the lives of others. Thank you, Betsey.

Along the way, others at Moody, like Janis Backing, and several colleagues at Huntington College, added helpful, timely comments that, little by little, gave shape to the manuscript and better prepared it to meet its readers. Alice and John Gordon led us to our miraculous Easter Sunday conversation with Dr. Ike Boruchow of Miami, Florida. Doctors and nurses, especially at Lutheran Hospital in Fort Wayne, but also at Indiana University Medical Center in Indianapolis, cared for Lizzie and me in ways that few who enter the world of advanced medicine may ever be privileged to encounter.

And, above all, I thank Lizzie, who, before there was a Betsey, helped me enormously to edit my thoughts. It is, of course, Lizzie's life and her example that inspired me to write the initial letters that became the foundation for this book; and it is Lizzie, too, who has felt the pain in reliving its events more keenly than I will ever know. She is my hero. I don't think I could ever stop finding more reasons to love her.

LETTERS FOR LIZZIE TEAM

ACQUIRING EDITOR
Mark Tobey

DEVELOPMENT EDITOR
Elizabeth Cody Newenhuyse

COPY EDITOR
Julie-Allyson Ieron, Joy Media

BACK COVER COPY
Elizabeth Cody Newenhuyse

COVER DESIGN
Ragont Design

COVER PHOTO
Susie Cushner/Images.com

INTERIOR DESIGN
Ragont Design

PRINTING AND BINDING
Versa Press, Inc.

The typeface for the text of this book is
Fournier MT